Elements of Literature®

Holt Adapted Reader

Instruction in Reading Literature and Related Texts

HOLT, RINEHART AND WINSTON

A Harcourt Education Company

Orlando • Austin • New York • San Diego • Toronto • London

Contents

Skills Table of Contents

A Book for You

Holt Adapted Reader is a book created especially for you. It is a size that's easy to carry around. This book actually tells you to write in it, circle, underline, and jot down responses. In addition to outstanding selections and background information, you'll find graphic organizers that encourage you to think a different way.

In *Holt Adapted Reader* you will find two kinds of selections—original literature and adaptations. Original literature is exactly what appears in *Elements of Literature*, Sixth Course. All the poems and plays in this book are examples of original literature. As you read original literature, you will find two kinds of help— **YOU NEED TO KNOW** and **IN OTHER WORDS**. You Need to Know gives you background information about the work. It also explains some of the work's main ideas. In Other Words paraphrases the text that comes before it. That is, it restates the text in different words.

Adaptations are based on stories or articles that appear in *Elements of Literature*, Sixth Course. Adaptations make the selections more accessible to all readers. You can easily identify any selection that is an adaptation. Just look for the words *based on* in the Table of Contents.

Holt Adapted Reader is designed to accompany *Elements of Literature*. Like *Elements of Literature*, it helps you interact with the literature and background materials. Here's what's in the book:

Reading Literature and Related Texts

When you read a historical essay, you read mainly to get information that is stated directly on the page. When you read literature, you need to go beyond the page. You need to read between the lines of a poem or story to discover the writer's meaning. No matter what kind of reading you do, *Holt Adapted Reader* will help you practice the skills and strategies you need to become an active and successful reader.

A Walk Through

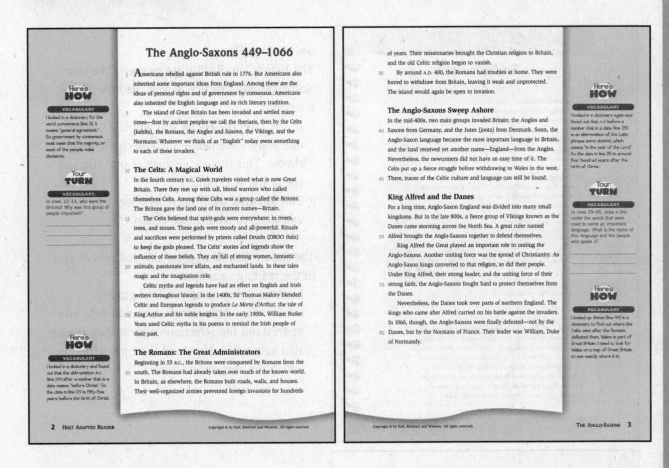

Historical Introductions

An introduction is provided for each literary period covered: the Anglo-Saxons, the Middle Ages, the Renaissance, the Restoration and the Eighteenth Century, the Romantic Period, the Victorian Period, and the Modern World: 1900 to the Present. Side notes focus on vocabulary terms. Each historical introduction ends with a list of key points to reinforce your understanding.

A Walk Through

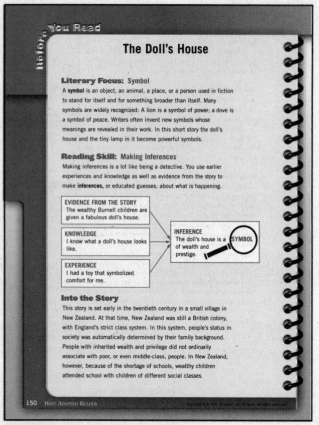

Before You Read

The Before You Read page previews the two skills you will practice as you read the selection.

- In the **Literary Focus** you will learn about one literary element—such as character or rhyme. This literary element is one you will see in the selection.
- The **Reading Skill** presents a key skill you will need to read the selection.

The Before You Read page also introduces you to the reading selection.

- **Into the Story** gives you background information. This information will help you understand the selection or its author. It may also help you understand the time period in which the story was written.

Interactive Selections from *Elements of Literature*

The literary selections you will read are from *Elements of Literature,* Sixth Course. Prose selections are adaptations. Poetry selections are original texts. The selections are reprinted to give you room to mark up the text.

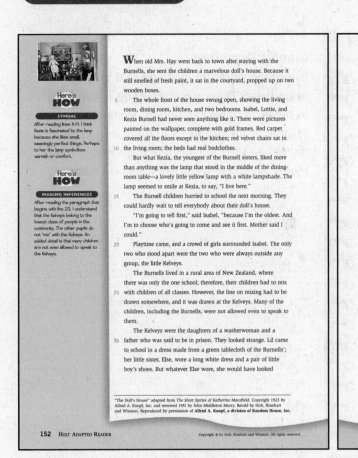

Strategies to Guide Your Reading: Side Notes

The **Here's How** feature models, or shows you, how to apply a particular skill to what you are reading. This feature lets you see how another person might think about the text. You can figure out the focus of a Here's How by looking in the red oval under the heading. Each Here's How focuses on a reading skill, a literary skill, or a vocabulary skill.

The **Your Turn** feature gives you a chance to practice a skill on your own. Each Your Turn focuses on a reading skill, a literary skill, or a vocabulary skill. You might be asked to underline or circle words in the text. You might also be asked to write your response to a question on lines that are provided for you.

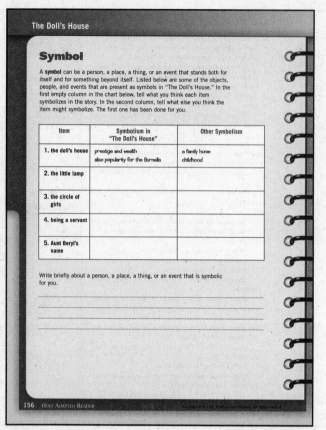

Graphic Organizers

After each selection, you will find **graphic organizers.** These pages give you a visual way to organize, interpret, and understand the reading or literary focus of the selection. You might be asked to chart the main events of the plot or complete a cause-and-effect chain.

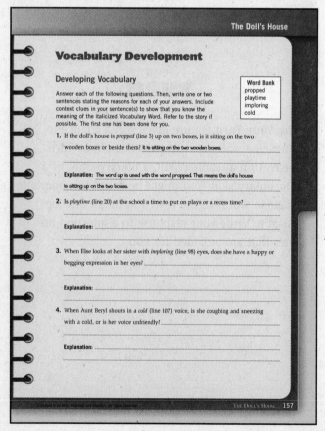

Vocabulary Development

Some selections are followed by **Vocabulary Development** worksheets. These worksheets check your understanding of the vocabulary in a selection. They also help you develop skills for vocabulary building.

Holt Adapted Reader

Instruction in Reading Literature and Related Texts

The Anglo-Saxons 449–1066

Americans rebelled against British rule in 1776. But Americans also inherited some important ideas from England. Among these are the ideas of personal rights and of government by consensus. Americans also inherited the English language and its rich literary tradition.

5 The island of Great Britain has been invaded and settled many times—first by ancient peoples we call the Iberians, then by the Celts (kehlts), the Romans, the Angles and Saxons, the Vikings, and the Normans. Whatever we think of as "English" today owes something to each of these invaders.

10 The Celts: A Magical World

In the fourth century B.C. Greek travelers visited what is now Great Britain. There they met up with tall, blond warriors who called themselves Celts. Among these Celts was a group called the Britons. The Britons gave the land one of its current names—Britain.

15 The Celts believed that spirit-gods were everywhere: in rivers, trees, and stones. These gods were moody and all-powerful. Rituals and sacrifices were performed by priests called Druids (DROO ihdz) to keep the gods pleased. The Celts' stories and legends show the influence of these beliefs. They are full of strong women, fantastic

20 animals, passionate love affairs, and enchanted lands. In these tales magic and the imagination rule.

Celtic myths and legends have had an effect on English and Irish writers throughout history. In the 1400s, Sir Thomas Malory blended Celtic and European legends to produce *Le Morte d'Arthur,* the tale of

25 King Arthur and his noble knights. In the early 1900s, William Butler Yeats used Celtic myths in his poems to remind the Irish people of their past.

The Romans: The Great Administrators

Beginning in 55 B.C., the Britons were conquered by Romans from the

30 south. The Romans had already taken over much of the known world. In Britain, as elsewhere, the Romans built roads, walls, and houses. Their well-organized armies prevented foreign invasions for hundreds

of years. Their missionaries brought the Christian religion to Britain, and the old Celtic religion began to vanish.

35   By around A.D. 400, the Romans had troubles at home. They were forced to withdraw from Britain, leaving it weak and unprotected. The island would again be open to invasion.

The Anglo-Saxons Sweep Ashore

In the mid-400s, two main groups invaded Britain: the Angles and
40 Saxons from Germany, and the Jutes (jootz) from Denmark. Soon, the Anglo-Saxon language became the most important language in Britain, and the land received yet another name—England—from the Angles. Nevertheless, the newcomers did not have an easy time of it. The Celts put up a fierce struggle before withdrawing to Wales in the west.
45 There, traces of the Celtic culture and language can still be found.

King Alfred and the Danes

For a long time, Anglo-Saxon England was divided into many small kingdoms. But in the late 800s, a fierce group of Vikings known as the Danes came storming across the North Sea. A great ruler named
50 Alfred brought the Anglo-Saxons together to defend themselves.

King Alfred the Great played an important role in uniting the Anglo-Saxons. Another uniting force was the spread of Christianity. As Anglo-Saxon kings converted to that religion, so did their people. Under King Alfred, their strong leader, and the uniting force of their
55 strong faith, the Anglo-Saxons fought hard to protect themselves from the Danes.

Nevertheless, the Danes took over parts of northern England. The kings who came after Alfred carried on his battle against the invaders. In 1066, though, the Anglo-Saxons were finally defeated—not by the
60 Danes, but by the Normans of France. Their leader was William, Duke of Normandy.

VOCABULARY

I looked in a dictionary again and found out that *a.d.* before a number that is a date (line 35) is an abbreviation of the Latin phrase *anno domini*, which means "in the year of the Lord." So the date in line 35 is around four hundred years after the birth of Christ.

VOCABULARY

In lines 39–45, draw a line under the words that were used to name an important language. What is the name of this language and the people who spoke it?

_____

_____

_____

VOCABULARY

I looked up *Wales* (line 44) in a dictionary to find out where the Celts went after the Romans defeated them. Wales is part of Great Britain. I need to look for Wales on a map of Great Britain to see exactly where it is.

Anglo-Saxon Life: The Warm Hall, the Cold World

The Anglo-Saxons were warriors, but they were not barbarians—that is, uncivilized. They crafted and used beautiful swords, helmets, cups,
65 jewelry, and coins.

But even more than riches, the Anglo-Saxons valued loyalty. Warfare and death were conditions of life. To survive, every group— whether family, tribe, or kingdom—depended on the strength of its leader. In return, the leader's followers offered him undying loyalty.
70 True loyalty, especially in war, was rewarded with gifts from the leader. It was also rewarded with fame. The epic hero Beowulf, for example, earns both glory and wealth by defending King Hrothgar against the monster Grendel.

Especially in winter, the Anglo-Saxon world was cold, dark, and
75 threatening. To protect themselves, the Anglo-Saxons lived close together. A group of small wooden homes usually surrounded a warm, fire-lit meeting hall. This arrangement helped the people in the community feel safe. It also meant that leaders and followers knew each other well. Such closeness meant that everyone could take part
80 when decisions had to be made.

The Anglo-Saxon Religion: Gods for Warriors

Despite the influence of Christianity, the old Anglo-Saxon religion did not disappear. This religion had come with the Anglo-Saxons from Germany, and it had much in common with what we think of as
85 Norse mythology. For example, the Norse gods Odin (OH dihn) and Thor appear in the Anglo-Saxon culture as Woden (WOH duhn) and Thunor. Woden (from which our *Wednesday*, or "Woden's Day," comes) is the god of death, poetry, and magic. He played an important part in a culture that produced great poetry and battled
90 daily against death. Thunor (who gave us a name for our *Thursday*) is the god of thunder and lightning. His sign is the hammer and possibly the twisted cross we call the swastika (SWOS tih kuh). This sign is found on many Anglo-Saxon gravestones.

Another key figure or element in Anglo-Saxon legend is the
95 dragon. The dragon is the protector of treasure. In Anglo-Saxon times

a dead warrior's ashes were buried alongside his riches. Some scholars believe that the dragon represents the guardian of the grave.

In general, the Anglo-Saxon religion was practical and useful. It focused on the down-to-earth values of bravery, loyalty, and
100 friendship.

The Bards: Singing of Gods and Heroes

The Anglo-Saxon meeting hall offered shelter and a place to hold meetings. During the long, dark evening hours, it was also used for entertainment. Poets, or bards, would sing to the strumming of a
105 harp. Their tales of gods and heroes charmed and delighted audiences who were tired of war, disease, and death. These tales provided a way for the Anglo-Saxons and their heroic deeds to be remembered after they died. It was the job of the bard to preserve a person's fame in song. Perhaps it was this power that earned the bards the favors and
110 rewards they enjoyed.

A Light in Ireland

Around A.D. 400, the remote island of Ireland was ignored by Germanic invaders—but not by a man named Patrick. Patrick was a Briton who had adopted the Roman way of life. When he was a
115 teenager, Celtic slave traders took Patrick to Ireland. Six years later, he escaped. After becoming a Christian bishop, he returned to Ireland, and in a few short years had converted the whole island to Christianity. Irish monks opened monasteries that became havens of learning. While the rest of Europe sank into constant warfare,
120 confusion, and ignorance, Ireland enjoyed a Golden Age.

The Christian Monasteries: The Ink Froze

Like the song of the bard—the poet and singer—Christianity also offered hope in the dark Anglo-Saxon world. As the bard preserved the memory of heroes, so the monasteries preserved the great Latin
125 and Greek myths and stories. They also preserved other popular works such as the epic poem *Beowulf*.

VOCABULARY

After reading lines 102–110, what do you think the word *bards* means? Draw a circle around the words in this paragraph that help you figure out the meaning.

_____

_____

_____

VOCABULARY

The word *havens* can mean harbors where ships can be anchored, or safe places. Which meaning does *havens* have in line 118? Underline the places that were havens.

_____

_____

_____

VOCABULARY

What is the meaning of the word *scribes* in line 127? What words and phrases in that paragraph help you figure out this meaning?

_____

_____

_____

_____

_____

VOCABULARY

I think the word *reign* in line 131 means the time when Alfred was king. The rest of the paragraph tells how King Alfred changed the language used by scholars from Latin to Anglo-Saxon while he was king.

Some of the monks who lived in monasteries were scribes. They spent most of the day in a writing room, copying texts by hand. The writing room was actually no more than a covered walkway; in 130 winter, the ink would sometimes freeze.

Until King Alfred's reign, Latin was the language of scholars and learning in England. But Alfred decided to have a history of England written in the Anglo-Saxon language. This work, the *Anglo-Saxon Chronicle,* helped to establish English as a language of learning and 135 culture. The Old English stories copied by the monks began to be seen and understood as great works of literature.

Key Features of the Anglo-Saxon Age

- Society was based on kinship, or groups of related people, led by a strong chief.
140 - People fought wars; farmed; governed; and created fine crafts.
- Christianity slowly replaced the old religion and linked England to Europe.
- Monasteries were centers of learning where monks wrote down works that had been passed on only by word of mouth for 145 centuries.
- English gained respect as a written language.

Kings and Queens of England

Bretwealdas

c. 477–491	Aelle, King of the West Saxons
c. 560–584	Caelwin, King of the West Saxons
584–616	Aethelbert, King of Kent
c. 600–616	Raedwald, King of East Anglia
616–632	Edwin, King of Northumbria
633–641	Oswald, King of Northumbria
654–670	Oswiu, King of Northumbria

King of Mercia

758–796	Offa

Kings of the West Saxons

802–839	Egbert
866–871	Aethelraed
871–899	Alfred
899–925	Edward the Elder
959–975	Edgar the Peaceable
979–1016	Aethelraed the Redeless
1016–1035	Cnut
1042–1066	Edward the Confessor
1066	Harold Godwinson

Normans

1066–1087	William I
1087–1100	William II
1100–1135	Henry I
1135–1154	Stephen

Angevins–Plantagenets

1154–1189	Henry II
1189–1199	Richard I
1199–1216	John
1216–1272	Henry III
1272–1307	Edward I
1307–1327	Edward II
1327–1377	Edward III
1377–1399	Richard II

House of Lancaster

1399–1413	Henry IV
1413–1422	Henry V
1422–1461	Henry VI

House of York

1461–1483	Edward IV
1483	Edward V
1483–1485	Richard III

House of Tudor

1485–1509	Henry VII
1509–1547	Henry VIII
1547–1553	Edward VI
1553–1558	Mary (I)
1558–1603	Elizabeth I

House of Stuart

1603–1625	James I
1625–1649	Charles I
1649–1660	Commonwealth and Protectorate
1660–1685	Charles II
1685–1688	James II
1688–1702	William III and Mary (II)
1702–1714	Anne

House of Hanover

1714–1727	George I
1727–1760	George II
1760–1820	George III
1820–1830	George IV
1830–1837	William IV
1837–1901	Victoria

House of Saxe-Coburg-Gotha

1901–1910	Edward VII
1910–1917	George V

House of Windsor

1917–1936	George V
1936	Edward VIII
1936–1952	George VI
1952–	Elizabeth II

The Battle with Grendel

Literary Focus: Epic Hero

The **epic hero** is the main character in a long narrative poem or a long story. In addition to great physical strength and ethical standards, epic heroes have all the qualities a particular group or society believes are heroic. In most **epics** the hero sets out on a quest, or journey, to save his people. Examples of epic heroes found in this reader are Beowulf, Gilgamesh, and Ulysses.

Reading Skill: Vocabulary

Some of the words used in this epic may seem strange to you. Some words may have **more than one meaning,** and you will have to read carefully to see which meaning a word has in the selection. You can figure out the meanings of some words by using **context clues**—the meanings of the words that surround them. Some words will be **archaic,** or very old. Archaic words are words no longer used in our speech today. Try to figure out the meanings of unfamiliar words on your own. Then, check a dictionary to see if you are correct.

Into the Epic

This is a story about a type of hero known as the dragon slayer. Beowulf, a hero of ancient England, faces violence, horror, and death to save his people from evil. He must battle Grendel, the monster lurking in the depths of the swamps. Grendel represents all the threatening monsters that heroes must slay. The epic takes place hundreds of years ago, but this story still has meaning for people today—perhaps because we live in a time when there is a need for a hero, a rescuer.

FROM
BEOWULF
The Battle with Grendel

TRANSLATED BY **Burton Raffel**

Statens Historiska Museer, Stockholm

Here's HOW

EPIC HERO

In lines 1–4, Grendel comes out of the bogs. He is full of hatred. God hates Grendel, too, so the monster must be evil and dangerous.

Your TURN

EPIC HERO

In lines 11–25, what words and phrases tell you that Grendel is a monster? Underline these words and phrases. Write the words you think are most vivid on the lines below.

_____

_____

_____

_____

_____

_____

_____

_____

_____

_____

_____

_____

YOU NEED TO KNOW   Grendel[1] attacked Herot, the home of the Danish King Hrothgar, and killed more than thirty of Hrothgar's men. After twelve years of Grendel's viciousness, Beowulf[2] comes to the aid of Hrothgar. Since Grendel uses no weapons, Beowulf asks to face the monster alone in hand-to-hand combat. The grateful Hrothgar accepts Beowulf's offer and gives a banquet in his honor. That night, Grendel heads toward Herot where, unknown to him, Beowulf and his men lie in wait.

Out from the marsh, from the foot of misty
Hills and bogs, bearing God's hatred,
Grendel came, hoping to kill
Anyone he could trap on this trip to high Herot.
5 He moved quickly through the cloudy night,
Up from his swampland, sliding silently
Toward that gold-shining hall. He had visited Hrothgar's
Home before, knew the way—
But never, before nor after that night,
10 Found Herot defended so firmly, his reception
So harsh. He journeyed, forever joyless,
Straight to the door, then snapped it open,
Tore its iron fasteners with a touch,
And rushed angrily over the threshold.
15 He strode quickly across the inlaid
Floor, snarling and fierce: His eyes
Gleamed in the darkness, burned with a gruesome
Light. Then he stopped, seeing the hall
Crowded with sleeping warriors, stuffed
20 With rows of young soldiers resting together.
And his heart laughed, he relished the sight,
Intended to tear the life from those bodies

---

1. **Grendel** (GREHN duhl).
2. **Beowulf** (BAY uh wulf).

By morning; the monster's mind was hot

With the thought of food and the feasting his belly

25 Would soon know. But fate, that night, intended

Grendel to gnaw the broken bones

Of his last human supper. Human

Eyes were watching his evil steps,

Waiting to see his swift hard claws.

30 Grendel snatched at the first Geat

He came to, ripped him apart, cut

His body to bits with powerful jaws,

Drank the blood from his veins, and bolted

Him down, hands and feet; death

35 And Grendel's great teeth came together,

Snapping life shut. Then he stepped to another

Still body, clutched at Beowulf with his claws,

Grasped at a strong-hearted wakeful sleeper

—And was instantly seized himself, claws

40 Bent back as Beowulf leaned up on one arm.

IN OTHER WORDS The monster Grendel comes up
from his swamp at night, thirsting after human blood.
Reaching Herot, the home of the Danish king and his
warriors, he rips the door from its hinges and enters the hall,
which is filled with sleeping warriors. Grendel grabs the first
soldier he sees and gobbles him down. Then the monster's
claws reach out for another warrior—but this warrior is
Beowulf, and he is ready.

That shepherd of evil, guardian of crime,

Knew at once that nowhere on earth

Had he met a man whose hands were harder;

His mind was flooded with fear—but nothing

45 Could take his talons and himself from that tight

Hard grip. Grendel's one thought was to run

From Beowulf, flee back to his marsh and hide there:

This was a different Herot than the hall he had emptied.

Here's HOW

VOCABULARY

In line 25, I figured out that fate is in control. Grendel is all set to eat up the warriors, but the poem says that fate meant this to be Grendel's last human supper. I think fate is some kind of power that controls the future.

Your TURN

EPIC HERO

Re-read lines 36–40, and underline the words that describe the actions of Beowulf.

Your TURN

VOCABULARY

The word *flooded* in line 44 can mean "overflowing with water" or "overwhelmed by a flow or movement of something." Which meaning do you think fits here? Why?

_____

_____

_____

_____

_____

_____

_____

_____

Statens Historiska Museer, Stockholm

But Higlac's[3] follower remembered his final

50 Boast and, standing erect, stopped
The monster's flight, fastened those claws
In his fists till they cracked, clutched Grendel
Closer. The infamous killer fought
For his freedom, wanting no flesh but retreat,

55 Desiring nothing but escape; his claws
Had been caught, he was trapped. That trip to Herot
Was a miserable journey for the writhing monster!
　　　The high hall rang, its roof boards swayed,
And Danes shook with terror. Down

60 The aisles the battle swept, angry
And wild. Herot trembled, wonderfully
Built to withstand the blows, the struggling
Great bodies beating at its beautiful walls;
Shaped and fastened with iron, inside

65 And out, artfully worked, the building
Stood firm. Its benches rattled, fell
To the floor, gold-covered boards grating
As Grendel and Beowulf battled across them.
Hrothgar's wise men had fashioned Herot

70 To stand forever; only fire,
They had planned, could shatter what such skill had put
Together, swallow in hot flames such splendor
Of ivory and iron and wood. Suddenly
The sounds changed, the Danes started

75 In new terror, cowering in their beds as the terrible
Screams of the Almighty's enemy sang
In the darkness, the horrible shrieks of pain
And defeat, the tears torn out of Grendel's
Taut[4] throat, hell's captive caught in the arms

80 Of him who of all the men on earth
Was the strongest.

---

3. **Higlac:** King of the Geats. "Higlac's follower" is Beowulf.
4. **taut** (tawt): stretched tight.

IN OTHER WORDS Beowulf has Grendel firmly in his powerful grasp, and the monster is terrified. Grendel had expected an easy meal. Now, all he wants to do is run home and hide. But Beowulf has sworn to kill Grendel with his bare hands, and he will not let the monster go. Their struggle shakes the strong walls of Herot. The soldiers shake with fear. Then a horrible scream rips through the night. It is Grendel.

EPIC HERO

Re-read lines 84–94. What prevented Beowulf's men from protecting him? Why was Beowulf alone successful against Grendel?

> That mighty protector of men
> Meant to hold the monster till its life
> Leaped out, knowing the fiend was no use
> To anyone in Denmark. All of Beowulf's
> 85 Band had jumped from their beds, ancestral
> Swords raised and ready, determined
> To protect their prince if they could. Their courage
> Was great but all wasted: They could hack at Grendel
> From every side, trying to open
> 90 A path for his evil soul, but their points
> Could not hurt him, the sharpest and hardest iron
> Could not scratch at his skin, for that sin-stained demon
> Had bewitched all men's weapons, laid spells
> That blunted every mortal man's blade.
> 95 And yet his time had come, his days
> Were over, his death near; down
> To hell he would go, swept groaning and helpless
> To the waiting hands of still worse fiends.
> Now he discovered—once the afflictor
> 100 Of men, tormentor of their days—what it meant
> To feud with Almighty God: Grendel
> Saw that his strength was deserting him, his claws
> Bound fast, Higlac's brave follower tearing at
> His hands. The monster's hatred rose higher,
> 105 But his power had gone. He twisted in pain,

Statens Historiska Museer, Stockholm

VOCABULARY

In lines 106–109, underline the words that describe the terrible injury that causes Grendel to lose the battle.

EPIC HERO

In stories about heroes, there is often some act that tells everyone that the hero has won. Read lines 124–126. What did Beowulf do to show everyone that he had killed Grendel?

_____

_____

_____

_____

And the bleeding sinews[5] deep in his shoulder

Snapped, muscle and bone split

And broke. The battle was over, Beowulf

Had been granted new glory: Grendel escaped,

110 But wounded as he was could flee to his den,

His miserable hole at the bottom of the marsh,

Only to die, to wait for the end

Of all his days. And after that bloody

Combat the Danes laughed with delight.

115 He who had come to them from across the sea,

Bold and strong-minded, had driven affliction

Off, purged Herot clean. He was happy,

Now, with that night's fierce work; the Danes

Had been served as he'd boasted he'd serve them; Beowulf,

120 A prince of the Geats, had killed Grendel,

Ended the grief, the sorrow, the suffering

Forced on Hrothgar's helpless people

By a bloodthirsty fiend. No Dane doubted

The victory, for the proof, hanging high

125 From the rafters where Beowulf had hung it, was the monster's

Arm, claw and shoulder and all.

IN OTHER WORDS Beowulf's men rush to his aid. However, Grendel is protected by a magic spell, and their swords cannot hurt him. Fortunately, their help is not needed. Grendel, trying to twist out of Beowulf's grip, feels his arm being ripped off. Mortally wounded, Grendel flees back to his swamp. Beowulf has rescued the Danes from the monster that tormented them. The victorious hero hangs the arm of Grendel from the rafters of the great hall.

And then, in the morning, crowds surrounded

Herot, warriors coming to that hall

From faraway lands, princes and leaders

130 Of men hurrying to behold the monster's

---

5. **sinews** (SIHN yooz): body tendons or connective tissue.

Great staggering tracks. They gaped with no sense

Of sorrow, felt no regret for his suffering,

Went tracing his bloody footprints, his beaten

And lonely flight, to the edge of the lake

135 Where he'd dragged his corpselike way, doomed

And already weary of his vanishing life.

The water was bloody, steaming and boiling

In horrible pounding waves, heat

Sucked from his magic veins; but the swirling

140 Surf had covered his death, hidden

Deep in murky darkness his miserable

End, as hell opened to receive him.

    Then old and young rejoiced, turned back

From that happy pilgrimage, mounted their hard-hooved

145 Horses, high-spirited stallions, and rode them

Slowly toward Herot again, retelling

Beowulf's bravery as they jogged along.

And over and over they swore that nowhere

On earth or under the spreading sky

150 Or between the seas, neither south nor north,

Was there a warrior worthier to rule over men.

(But no one meant Beowulf's praise to belittle

Hrothgar, their kind and gracious king!) . . .

IN OTHER WORDS The next morning, crowds of people begin to arrive from far away, eager to see the place where Grendel was defeated. They follow his bloody footprints to the lake where he went down to his death. Beowulf is a hero, and there is great rejoicing.

Statens Historiska Museer, Stockholm

Your
TURN

VOCABULARY

Re-read lines 140–142, and tell what you think the word *murky* in line 141 means. What other words in these lines help you with the meaning?

_____

_____

_____

Your
TURN

EPIC HERO

Underline the phrase in lines 149–151 that best describes Beowulf as a hero.

Epic Hero

The **epic hero** is the main character in a long narrative poem or a long story. The hero has all the qualities a particular group or society believes are heroic. In *Beowulf* the hero is often described with rich imagery—word-pictures that appeal to the senses. In each of the items below, re-read the lines from the selection, and then write the words from the narrative that vividly bring out, or emphasize, Beowulf's heroism. The first one has been done for you.

1. **Read lines 42–43:**

   "nowhere on earth / Had he met a man whose hands were harder . . ."

   _____

2. **Read lines 116–117:**

   _____

   _____

3. **Read lines 146–151:**

   _____

   _____

Answer the question below:

- What specific character traits do the images you have listed reveal about Beowulf? Explain how the images you have listed show that Beowulf is an **epic hero.**

   _____

   _____

   _____

   _____

   _____

Vocabulary Development

Anglo-Saxon Words and Word Parts

English has borrowed words from most of the world's languages, but many words in our basic vocabulary come to us from Anglo-Saxon, or Old English.

Study the chart below. Then, list examples of modern English words that use each of the Anglo-Saxon prefixes shown.

Prefixes from Anglo-Saxon	Meanings	Examples
a–	in; on; of; up; to	afloat, aside
be–	around; about; treat as	behind, begin
for–	away; off; from	forget
mis–	badly; not; wrongly	misspell, misfire
over–	above; excessive	overtake, oversee
un–	not; reverse of	untrue, unknown

Examples: _____

_____

_____

_____

from Gilgamesh: A Verse Narrative

Literary Focus: Conflict

A **conflict** is a struggle or clash between opposing characters, forces, or emotions.

Character vs. Character

Beowulf fighting Grendel

Character(s) vs. Outside Force

Passengers on Titanic *vs. Iceberg*

CONFLICT

Groups vs. Groups

Democrats vs. Republicans

Character vs. Inner Self

Humbaba vs. Fear of Dying

Many works contain more than one kind of conflict.

Reading Skill: Responding to the Text

Take notes as you read the epic or as someone reads it aloud. You may want to describe the images you see. You may have questions about the characters or about what happens in the story. Writing down your reactions to the story, the characters, and the events is important because it helps you to better understand the text.

Into the Epic

Gilgamesh (GIL gah mehsh) was an actual king of Uruk, in Babylonia, between 2700 and 2500 B.C. Over time, legends grew up about Gilgamesh, and he became a superhuman figure. In the excerpt you are about to read, Gilgamesh and his friend Enkidu have decided to confront the evil guardian of the cedar forest, the monster Humbaba. Gilgamesh makes Humbaba come out and fight by cutting down a cedar tree, which is sacred and holy to the monster.

FROM

Gilgamesh:

A Verse Narrative

Retold by

Herbert Mason

YOU NEED TO KNOW   Gilgamesh, who is two-thirds god and one-third human, is handsome, courageous, and strong. He also rules unfairly at times. Gilgamesh's people pray to the gods for relief from his mistreatment. In response, the gods send a match for Gilgamesh: the wild man Enkidu (EHN kee doo), raised by animals and not used to living with people. After a wrestling match, Gilgamesh and Enkidu become close friends and together they go on a series of adventures. They plan a journey to the cedar forest where they will confront the evil giant Humbaba. As this part of the story opens, Gilgamesh is striking the blow that will lure Humbaba out of the forest.

At dawn Gilgamesh raised his ax
And struck at the great cedar.
When Humbaba heard the sound of falling trees,
He hurried down the path that they had seen
5 But only he had traveled. Gilgamesh felt weak
At the sound of Humbaba's footsteps and called to Shamash[1]
Saying, I have followed you in the way decreed;
Why am I abandoned now? Suddenly the winds
Sprang up. They saw the great head of Humbaba
10 Like a water buffalo's bellowing down the path,
His huge and clumsy legs, his flailing[2] arms
Thrashing at phantoms in his precious trees.
His single stroke could cut a cedar down
And leave no mark on him. His shoulders,
15 Like a porter's[3] under building stones,
Were permanently bent by what he bore;
He was the slave who did the work for gods
But whom the gods would never notice.

---

1. **Shamash** (SHAH mahsh): the sun god. The god has been guiding Gilgamesh.
2. **flailing**: swinging.
3. **porter's**: A porter is a person who carries things.

Monstrous in his contortion, he aroused

20 The two almost to pity.

But pity was the thing that might have killed.

It made them pause just long enough to show

How pitiless he was to them. Gilgamesh in horror saw

Him strike the back of Enkidu and beat him to the ground

25 Until he thought his friend was crushed to death.

He stood still watching as the monster leaned to make

His final strike against his friend, unable

To move to help him, and then Enkidu slid

Along the ground like a ram making its final lunge

30 On wounded knees. Humbaba fell and seemed

To crack the ground itself in two, and Gilgamesh,

As if this fall had snapped him from his daze,

Returned to life

And stood over Humbaba with his ax

35 Raised high above his head watching the monster plead

In strangled sobs and desperate appeals

The way the sea contorts under a violent squall.[4]

I'll serve you as I served the gods, Humbaba said;

I'll build you houses from their sacred trees.

40 Enkidu feared his friend was weakening

And called out: Gilgamesh! Don't trust him!

As if there were some hunger in himself

That Gilgamesh was feeling

That turned him momentarily to yearn

45 For someone who would serve, he paused;

And then he raised his ax up higher

And swung it in a perfect arc

Into Humbaba's neck. He reached out

To touch the wounded shoulder of his friend,

50 And late that night he reached again

To see if he was yet asleep, but there was only

---

4. **squall:** sudden, brief storm.

RESPONDING TO THE TEXT

Re-read lines 34–45. At this point in the story, what notes might you make about what is happening?

_____

_____

_____

_____

_____

_____

_____

Your TURN

CONFLICT

Re-read lines 35–39. What is Humbaba offering to Gilgamesh in an attempt to save himself? How does this conflict with, or go against, what Gilgamesh wants to do?

_____

_____

_____

_____

_____

_____

RESPONDING TO THE TEXT

What do you think of the ending of the story of the attack on Humbaba? Explain your answer.

_____

_____

_____

_____

_____

_____

_____

_____

Quiet breathing. The stars against the midnight sky
Were sparkling like mica[5] in a riverbed.
In the slight breeze
55 The head of Humbaba was swinging from a tree.

IN OTHER WORDS Gilgamesh goes to cut down a cedar tree. The monster Humbaba hears the sound of the ax and rushes toward Gilgamesh and Enkidu. When the two men see the deformed monster, slave to the gods, they almost feel pity and do not attack immediately. Humbaba attacks first and nearly kills Enkidu. Frozen with horror, Gilgamesh looks on as Humbaba aims a final blow. Just in time, Enkidu drags himself out of the way, and Humbaba falls. Gilgamesh snaps out of his daze and raises his ax to kill the monster. Humbaba pleads for his life, offering to serve Gilgamesh instead of the gods. Gilgamesh pauses, as if tempted, but Enkidu cries out not to trust Humbaba. Gilgamesh raises his ax again and chops off the monster's head.

---

5. **mica** (MY kuh): colored, translucent mineral.

Conflict

A **conflict** is a struggle or clash between opposing characters, forces, or emotions.

In an **external** conflict, a character fights against some outside force. An example is one character fighting against another, as in the story of Beowulf's battle with Grendel. Characters may have to battle a natural force, such as a storm or a collision with an iceberg. The conflict can also be between groups, as in a war.

An **internal** conflict happens inside a person or character. This is when a character has opposing, or conflicting, needs, desires, or emotions.

In the chart below, list the conflicts faced by Gilgamesh, Enkidu, and Humbaba in "The Head of Humbaba." Give the quotation or words that describe the conflict. Then, tell whether each conflict is **external** or **internal**. Some have been done for you.

Gilgamesh	Enkidu	Humbaba
Lines 34–35 "Stood over Humbaba with his ax raised high above his head watching the monster plead" External	**Lines 19–20**	**Lines 3–4** "When Humbaba heard the sound of falling trees, he hurried down the path." External
Lines 42–45	**Lines 24–25** "strike the back of Enkidu and beat him to the ground" "crushed to death" External	**Lines 24–30**

The Middle Ages 1066–1485

In October 1066, a daylong battle was fought near the channel of water that divides England from France. In that battle, Duke William of Normandy, France, defeated Harold, the last of the Anglo-Saxon kings. This began the Norman Conquest.

5   William fought to win the English throne because he believed it was rightfully his. The previous Anglo-Saxon king, Edward the Confessor, was a relative of William's. When King Edward died, William claimed that Edward had promised him the crown. When Harold was made king instead, William led an enormous army across 10 the English Channel and won the crown for his own.

Under William, England became more like the countries on the continent of Europe. French was the language spoken in William's court and by the nobles, although English was still spoken by the ordinary people. William divided English land among his own 15 followers. These men brought a social system known as feudalism from Europe to England.

Feudalism and Knighthood: Pyramid Power

Feudalism was like a pyramid of power. The king sat at the top of the pyramid. He appointed barons—noblemen—to serve him as his 20 vassals. The barons gave the king money, military support, or both. The barons, in turn, chose vassals of their own—and so on down the pyramid. At the bottom were serfs—laborers who were like slaves— who were not free to leave the nobleman or his land.

The feudal system did not always work. Sometimes a vassal 25 would switch his loyalty to a more powerful lord, and battles would follow. Indeed, we cannot think of the Middle Ages without thinking of knights in armor. Expected to serve as warriors, most males (other than serfs) began training for the knighthood at an early age. Once knighted, a youth became a man with the title "Sir."

30   Knights had to behave according to a strict code known as chivalry. This code was based on loyalty, bravery, and courtly behavior. Breaking one of the code's rules would weaken the knight's position—and the whole of knighthood itself.

VOCABULARY

I think vassals (line 20) must be people who were like servants to the people who were more powerful. I have read lines 17 to 23, and it looks to me like everyone was a vassal to the king.

VOCABULARY

I know that *code* means "secret writing" but in line 30, it means "set of rules." The word *rules* in line 32 helped me understand this.

Women in Medieval Society: No Voice, No Choice

35 Women had no political rights under feudalism. A woman had to depend entirely on a man, whether husband, father, or brother. For peasant women, life was a tiring round of childbearing and working in the fields and around the house. Women of higher rank spent their time raising children and managing their households. If the men

40 were away at war, such women might also govern the estate—but only until the men came home.

Chivalry and Courtly Love: Ideal but Unreal

The code of chivalry ruled how a knight must behave toward his lord and toward his enemy. It also dictated how he must behave toward

45 women. Courtly love—the practice of adoring a worthy lady—was thought to make the knight braver and better. Ideally, this love was not sexual. A knight's ideal woman always remained pure and out of reach. The resulting tension gave poets and storytellers plenty of drama to work with.

50 Under chivalry, women became idealized objects—perfect in every way. In fact, the code and practice of chivalry brought about a new form of literature—the romance. However, it did little to improve the actual lives of women.

The New City Classes: Out from Under the Overlords

55 Society in the Middle Ages centered on the feudal castle. But as England's population grew, so did its towns and cities. The people of the cities were free, tied neither to the land and its owner nor to knighthood and chivalry. These people appear in the works of Geoffrey Chaucer. Living in cities such as London and Canterbury, his

60 characters are not defined by feudalism but by the work that they do. The new merchant class had its own money and its own tastes in the arts. Therefore, much art from this time reflects the lives and interests of the middle class.

The Great Happenings

65 Against the backdrop of feudalism, several major events changed the course of English history and literature.

VOCABULARY

What do you think the word *chivalry* (lines 42–43) means? What other word in line 42 helps you figure out the meaning? Look back to lines 30–33 for more help with the meaning.

_____

_____

_____

_____

VOCABULARY

I know that a merchant is someone who buys and sells things. So the "merchant class" (line 61) must be the class, or group of people, who buy and sell things.

VOCABULARY

Does the word *course* in line 66 mean "a series of studies," or does it mean "the direction that something takes"? What clues in the text help you understand this word?

_____

_____

_____

_____

The Crusades

In Chaucer's *The Canterbury Tales* we meet a knight who has fought in "heathen" places. His adventures in the 1300s were really an
70 extension of the Crusades (1095–1270). In this series of so-called holy wars, European Christians tried to conquer the Muslims of the Middle East. Although the Crusades were a military failure, they brought together people from Europe and the East. Contact with eastern mathematics, astronomy, and art enriched European culture—and
75 made possible the lively world of Chaucer.

The Martyrdom of Thomas à Becket

When Chaucer's pilgrims set out for Canterbury, their goal was the shrine of Saint Thomas à Becket (c. 1118–1170). Becket, a Norman, had risen to power under King Henry II (reigned 1154–1189). At that
80 time, all Christians belonged to the Church of Rome. Even King Henry was a vassal—or servant—of the pope, the powerful head of the Church in Rome. However, Henry hoped to take on some of the power of Rome. To help do this, he gave his friend Thomas the most powerful church position in England. The plan backfired, though,
85 as Becket was independent-minded and often took the pope's side. This enraged Henry and gave four of his loyal knights the idea of murdering Becket in his own cathedral. Becket became a martyr—someone who dies for his or her beliefs—and Henry's power against the pope in Rome was weakened.

90   The power of the Church had both good and bad effects. At its worst, some priests and other clergy misused their powers. In Chaucer's *The Canterbury Tales,* for example, the Monk lives a life of luxury, and the Friar chases women. But the Church also brought together all the nations and peoples of Europe. The Church continued
95 to be the center of learning, as well, and Latin remained the language of educated Europeans.

The Magna Carta: Power to (Some of) the People

In 1215, a group of English barons forced King John to sign the Magna Carta, or "Great Charter." This document emphasized the
100 rights of common people and later became the basis for much of

English law. At the time, though, the barons did not care about commoners. They wanted to use the Magna Carta to curb the power of the king—which it did.

The Hundred Years' War (1337–1453)

105 This war, fought in Europe, was based on claims to the French throne by two English kings, Edward III and Henry V. England lost the war but gained a new society in the process. Most English armies in France were made up of small landowners, or yeomen. These landowner-warriors now became an important force in English

110 society. Chivalry and knighthood faded into the past, and a new, democratic England was born.

The Black Death

The Black Death, or bubonic plague, struck England in 1348–1349. Spread by fleas carried on rats, this disease was easy to catch and

115 killed off one third of England's population. It also created a labor shortage and gave the lower classes more power than ever before. One long-term effect was the serfs' freedom—and with that came the end of feudalism.

The Middle Ages: Four Centuries of Change

- The Norman Conquest brought England into mainstream Europe.
- The feudal system was a pyramid of loyalty with the king on top.
- The Roman Church brought Europeans together under one faith.
- The rise of towns and cities freed people from feudalism and created a new way of life.
- The Magna Carta weakened the power of the king and formed a basis for later English laws.
- The Crusades linked Europe to the East and enriched European culture.
- Women were honored under chivalry but not granted any rights.
- The rise of the yeoman class paved the way for democracy.
- The Black Death created a labor shortage that helped end feudalism.

Your
TURN

VOCABULARY

The word *curb* in line 102 can mean "to hold back" or "concrete edge." Which of these meanings do you think *curb* has in lines 102–103? Explain your answer.

_____

_____

_____

_____

_____

_____

_____

_____

from The Canterbury Tales

Literary Focus: Characterization

Characterization is the way a writer shows the personality of a
character. For example, Chaucer *tells* us that the Knight "was a true,
a perfect gentle-knight." This is **direct** characterization. He also
reveals his characters by telling us

- how the character looks and dresses
- how the character speaks and acts
- what the character thinks and feels
- how others respond to the character

Reading Skill: Analyzing Key Details

With twenty-nine characters to introduce, Chaucer could not develop
any character at great length. He gives the reader a few well-chosen
key details that make each character stand out vividly. Here is how
Chaucer describes the Nun (see page 33): "Her nose was elegant,
her eyes glass-gray; / Her mouth was very small, but soft and
red, . . ."

Into the Poem

In Chaucer's day almost everyone—rich and poor—made a
pilgrimage, or journey to a sacred place. The purpose of a pilgrimage
to Canterbury was to visit St. Thomas à Becket's shrine in the
cathedral there. The way from London to Canterbury was originally a
Roman road. You can still travel on parts of this road today. However,
the hayfields and forests have all disappeared. So has the deep mud
that filled the road in April, when these pilgrims were traveling to
Canterbury.

FROM THE PROLOGUE TO

The Canterbury Tales

Geoffrey Chaucer

TRANSLATED BY **Nevill Coghill**

YOU NEED TO KNOW The Prologue, or introduction, to *The Canterbury Tales* introduces the twenty-nine pilgrims who, along with the narrator, are on their way to the shrine of St. Thomas à Becket in Canterbury. The time is April, and the place is The Tabard Inn, just outside London, where the pilgrims are staying overnight. The narrator describes each of the pilgrims, revealing their personalities. He promises that he will repeat what he sees and hears during the pilgrimage, no matter what. Finally he describes the Host's proposal that each pilgrim tell two tales on the way and two on the return. In the following selections from The Prologue, you will meet eight of the twenty-nine pilgrims, as described by the narrator.

Here's HOW

CHARACTERIZATION

From reading the first four lines, I get a good idea of what kind of a man the knight is. He is distinguished, has good manners, believes in truth and honor, and is generous and courteous.

Here's HOW

VOCABULARY

I think the word *heathen* in line 7 means the opposite of "Christian" because these two words are compared. Christianity is one kind of religion. I think *heathen* means "having no religion." I checked in a dictionary, and that is one definition of *heathen*.

The Knight

There was a *Knight*, a most distinguished man,
Who from the day on which he first began
To ride abroad had followed chivalry,
Truth, honor, generousness, and courtesy.
5 He had done nobly in his sovereign's war
And ridden into battle, no man more,
As well in Christian as in heathen places,
And ever honored for his noble graces.
　　When we took Alexandria,[1] he was there.
10 He often sat at table in the chair
Of honor, above all nations, when in Prussia.
In Lithuania he had ridden, and Russia,
No Christian man so often, of his rank.
When, in Granada, Algeciras sank
15 Under assault, he had been there, and in

---

1. Alexandria: city in Egypt captured by the Crusaders in 1365. In the next few lines, Chaucer is indicating the knight's distinguished and extensive career.

From "The Prologue" from *The Canterbury Tales* by Geoffrey Chaucer, translated by Nevill Coghill (Penguin Classics 1951, Fourth Revised Edition 1977). Copyright 1951 by Nevill Coghill; copyright renewed © 1958, 1960, 1975, 1977 by the Estate of Nevill Coghill. Reproduced by permission of **Penguin Books Ltd.**

North Africa, raiding Benamarin;

In Anatolia he had been as well

And fought when Ayas and Attalia fell,

For all along the Mediterranean coast

20　He had embarked with many a noble host.

In fifteen mortal battles he had been

And jousted for our faith at Tramissene

Thrice in the lists, and always killed his man.

This same distinguished knight had led the van

25　Once with the Bey of Balat, doing work

For him against another heathen Turk;

He was of sovereign value in all eyes.

And though so much distinguished, he was wise

And in his bearing modest as a maid.

30　He never yet a boorish thing had said

In all his life to any, come what might;

He was a true, a perfect gentle-knight.[2]

　　　Speaking of his equipment, he possessed

Fine horses, but he was not gaily dressed.

35　He wore a fustian[3] tunic stained and dark

With smudges where his armor had left mark;

Just home from service, he had joined our ranks

To do his pilgrimage and render thanks.

IN OTHER WORDS　The first pilgrim is the Knight, who has a long military career. He has taken part in battles in Europe and Africa and been victorious in all of them. The Knight is described as truthful, honorable, generous, well mannered, noble, and wise. He does not brag or boast about his achievements. Although he has fine horses—a mark of his wealth—he does not show off in fancy clothes. Instead, he wears a simple long coat, still stained from being worn under his armor. He has just come back from the war, and he is eager to give thanks to God.

---

2. **gentle-knight:** In Chaucer's day, *gentle* meant "well bred and considerate."
3. **fustian** (FUHS chuhn): coarse cloth made of linen and cotton.

Here's HOW

ANALYZING KEY DETAILS

In lines 21–23, I see that the Knight fought in fifteen battles, jousted three times at a place called Tramissene, and always killed his man. These details help me see the Knight as a brave and skillful fighter. I would want to be on the Knight's side in a battle.

Your TURN

CHARACTERIZATION

In lines 33–36, what do the details of the Knight's equipment and clothing tell you about his character?

_____

_____

_____

Your TURN

VOCABULARY

What is the meaning of the word *render* in line 38? Look at line 37 and "In Other Words" for "The Knight" for clues that will help you figure out the meaning.

_____

_____

_____

Your
TURN

ANALYZING KEY DETAILS

What details about the Nun in lines 41–47 suggest that the narrator does not like her and thinks that she is trying to appear more refined and "high class" than she really is?

_____

_____

_____

_____

_____

_____

Your
TURN

CHARACTERIZATION

What do the table manners of the Nun in lines 48–57 tell you about her character?

_____

_____

_____

_____

_____

_____

_____

_____

_____

_____

The Nun

There also was a *Nun*, a Prioress,

40 Her way of smiling very simple and coy.

Her greatest oath was only "By St. Loy!"[4]

And she was known as Madam Eglantyne.[5]

And well she sang a service, with a fine

Intoning through her nose, as was most seemly,

45 And she spoke daintily in French, extremely,

After the school of Stratford-atte-Bowe[6]

French in the Paris style she did not know.

At meat her manners were well taught withal;

No morsel from her lips did she let fall,

50 Nor dipped her fingers in the sauce too deep;

But she could carry a morsel up and keep

The smallest drop from falling on her breast.

For courtliness she had a special zest,

And she would wipe her upper lip so clean

55 That not a trace of grease was to be seen

Upon the cup when she had drunk; to eat,

She reached a hand sedately for the meat.

She certainly was very entertaining,

Pleasant and friendly in her ways, and straining

60 To counterfeit a courtly kind of grace,

A stately bearing fitting to her place,

And to seem dignified in all her dealings.

As for her sympathies and tender feelings,

She was so charitably solicitous

65 She used to weep if she but saw a mouse

Caught in a trap, if it were dead or bleeding.

And she had little dogs she would be feeding

With roasted flesh, or milk, or fine white bread.

And bitterly she wept if one were dead

---

4. St. Loy: Saint Eligius, known for his perfect manners.

5. Eglantyne: a kind of a rose and also the name of several romantic heroines. The Nun herself is a romantic.

6. Stratford-atte-Bowe: Benedictine convent near London where inferior French was spoken.

70 Or someone took a stick and made it smart;

She was all sentiment and tender heart.

Her veil was gathered in a seemly way,

Her nose was elegant, her eyes glass-gray;

Her mouth was very small, but soft and red,

75 Her forehead, certainly, was fair of spread,

Almost a span[7] across the brows, I own;

She was indeed by no means undergrown.

Her cloak, I noticed, had a graceful charm.

She wore a coral trinket on her arm,

80 A set of beads, the gaudies tricked in green,[8]

Whence hung a golden brooch of brightest sheen

On which there first was graven a crowned A,

And lower, *Amor vincit omnia*.[9]

IN OTHER WORDS   The Nun is very different from the
Knight. Although she is a sister in a religious order, she
wants to appear polite, dainty, and well mannered. In fact,
she loves to show off. When she takes part in a religious
service, she is thinking not of God but of her own singing.
She speaks French but not very well; she is greatly concerned
with table manners. She shows off her love for animals and
spoils her little pet dogs. The Nun is plump, has a small
mouth and a wide forehead, and wears a rather showy set of
coral prayer beads.

The Monk

A *Monk* there was, one of the finest sort

85 Who rode the country; hunting was his sport.

A manly man, to be an Abbott able;

Many a dainty horse he had in stable.

---

7. **span:** nine inches.
8. **a set of beads . . . green:** Beads are a rosary, or prayer beads and a crucifix on a string or
   chain. Every eleventh bead is a gaud, a large bead indicating when the Lord's Prayer is to
   be said.
9. ***Amor vincit omnia*** (AH mawr WIHN kiht AWM nee uh): Latin for "Love conquers all."

Your TURN

ANALYZING KEY DETAILS

In lines 73–77, read the details that describe the Nun. Do you think she has a pretty face? Give one detail about her face that supports your answer.

Here's HOW

CHARACTERIZATION

In lines 94–95, I have underlined where the narrator comes right out and says that the Monk does not like old-fashioned things but prefers the modern world's less strict ways. This is called direct characterization.

Your TURN

CHARACTERIZATION

A monk is a member of a religious order who has taken vows of poverty, chastity, and obedience. In lines 96–116, how do the details describing the Monk suggest, without directly saying it, that this Monk is not serious about his vows?

_____

_____

_____

_____

_____

_____

_____

_____

_____

His bridle, when he rode, a man might hear

Jingling in a whistling wind as clear,

90 Aye, and as loud as does the chapel bell

Where my lord Monk was Prior of the cell.

The Rule of good St. Benet or St. Maur[10]

As old and strict he tended to ignore;

<u>He let go by the things of yesterday</u>

95 And <u>took the modern world's more spacious way.</u>

He did not rate that text at a plucked hen

Which says that hunters are not holy men

And that a monk uncloistered is a mere

Fish out of water, flapping on the pier,

100 That is to say a monk out of his cloister.

That was a text he held not worth an oyster;

And I agreed and said his views were sound;

Was he to study till his head went round

Poring over books in cloisters? Must he toil

105 As Austin[11] bade and till the very soil?

Was he to leave the world upon the shelf?

Let Austin have his labor to himself.

    This Monk was therefore a good man to horse;

Greyhounds he had, as swift as birds, to course.[12]

110 Hunting a hare or riding at a fence

Was all his fun, he spared for no expense.

I saw his sleeves were garnished at the hand

With fine gray fur, the finest in the land,

And on his hood, to fasten it at his chin

115 He had a wrought-gold, cunningly fashioned pin;

Into a lover's knot it seemed to pass.

<u>His head was bald and shone like looking-glass;</u>

<u>So did his face,</u> as if it had been greased.

---

10. St. Benet [Benedict] **or St. Maur** [Maurice]: Saint Benedict (c. 480–c. 547) was an Italian monk who founded numerous monasteries and wrote a famous code of regulations for monastic life. Saint Maurice was a follower of Benedict.

11. Austin: Saint Augustine (354–430), bishop of Hippo in North Africa. He criticized lazy monks and suggested they do some hard manual labor.

12. course: to cause to chase game.

He was a fat and personable priest;
120 His prominent eyeballs never seemed to settle.
They glittered like the flames beneath a kettle;
Supple his boots, his horse in fine condition.
He was a prelate fit for exhibition,
He was not pale like a tormented soul.
125 He liked a fat swan best, and roasted whole.
His palfrey[13] was as brown as is a berry.

IN OTHER WORDS Like the Nun, the Monk is rather worldly for a religious person. He does not shut himself away in his monastery to study and work; he considers such a life strict and old-fashioned. Instead, he loves to ride out hunting—not at all traditional for a monk. He spends a lot of money on his hobby, and he has many fine horses and hunting dogs. The Monk adorns himself with fur and gold, and he enjoys such extravagant dishes as whole roasted swan. He is fat and bald, with a shiny face.

The Oxford Cleric

An *Oxford Cleric,* still a student though,
One who had taken logic long ago,
Was there; his horse was thinner than a rake,
130 And he was not too fat, I undertake,
But had a hollow look, a sober stare;
The thread upon his overcoat was bare.
He had found no preferment in the church
And he was too unworldly to make search
135 For secular employment. By his bed
He preferred having twenty books in red
And black, of Aristotle's[14] philosophy,
Than costly clothes, fiddle, or psaltery.[15]

---

13. **palfrey:** horse.
14. **Aristotle's** (AR ih sтот uhl): Aristotle (384–322 B.C.) was a Greek philosopher.
15. **psaltery** (SAWL tuhr ee): a stringed instrument that is plucked.

Your **TURN**

ANALYZING KEY DETAILS

What details in lines 132–138 fit the popular stereotype of the starving student?

_____

_____

_____

_____

_____

_____

_____

_____

_____

_____

_____

Though a philosopher, as I have told,
140 He had not found the stone for making gold.[16]
Whatever money from his friends he took
He spent on learning or another book
And prayed for them most earnestly, returning
Thanks to them thus for paying for his learning.
145 His only care was study, and indeed
He never spoke a word more than was need,
Formal at that, respectful in the extreme,
Short, to the point, and lofty in his theme.
A tone of moral virtue filled his speech
150 And gladly would he learn, and gladly teach.

IN OTHER WORDS The Oxford Cleric is a thin, quiet, serious-looking man; his coat is almost worn out; even his horse is underfed. He has no profession, and he spends all his time studying. If his friends give him money, he spends it on another book instead of food or clothes, and he repays them by praying for them.

The Doctor

A *Doctor* too emerged as we proceeded;
No one alive could talk as well as he did
On points of medicine and of surgery,
For, being grounded in astronomy,
155 He watched his patient closely for the hours
When, by his horoscope, he knew the powers
Of favorable planets, then ascendent,
Worked on the images for his dependent.
The cause of every malady you'd got

Here's HOW

CHARACTERIZATION

In lines 151-153, we are told that the Doctor talks very well. This is direct characterization.

---

16. stone . . . gold: Alchemists at the time were searching for a stone that was supposed to turn ordinary metals into gold.

160 He knew, and whether dry, cold, moist, or hot;[17]

He knew their seat, their humor and condition.

He was a perfect practicing physician.

These causes being known for what they were,

He gave the man his medicine then and there.

165 All his apothecaries in a tribe

Were ready with the drugs he would prescribe

And each made money from the other's guile;

They had been friendly for a goodish while.

He was well-versed in Aesculapius[18] too

170 And what Hippocrates and Rufus knew

And Dioscorides, now dead and gone,

Galen and Rhazes, Hali, Serapion,

Averroes, Avicenna, Constantine,

Scotch Bernard, John of Gaddesden, Gilbertine.

175 In his own diet he observed some measure;

There were no superfluities for pleasure,

Only digestives, nutritives and such.

He did not read the Bible very much.

In blood-red garments, slashed with bluish gray

180 And lined with taffeta, he rode his way;

Yet he was rather close as to expenses

And kept the gold he won in pestilences.

Gold stimulates the heart, or so we're told.

He therefore had a special love of gold.

IN OTHER WORDS   The Doctor appears to know a great deal about medieval medicine. He has studied medical writings from ancient times. He treats patients using astronomy and the four "humors." The narrator thinks the Doctor is more interested in making money by prescribing treatments his patients do not need than in actually helping his patients.

---

17. **dry . . . hot:** the four humors, or fluids. People of the time believed that one's physical and mental conditions were influenced by the balance of four major fluids in the body—blood (hot and wet), yellow bile (hot and dry), phlegm (cold and wet), and black bile (cold and dry).

18. **Aesculapius** (ehs kyuh LAY pee uhs): in Greek and Roman mythology, the god of medicine. The names that follow were early Greek, Roman, Middle Eastern, and medieval medical authorities.

ANALYZING KEY DETAILS

Re-read lines 160–164. What do the details in these lines tell you about the Doctor?

_____

_____

_____

_____

_____

_____

Your TURN

VOCABULARY

The word *guile* (gyl) in line 167 means "sly dealings." What does the use of this word here tell you about the Doctor and the apothecaries?

_____

_____

_____

_____

_____

_____

_____

_____

_____

The Wife of Bath

185　**A** worthy *woman* from beside *Bath* city

Was with us, somewhat deaf, which was a pity.

In making cloth she showed so great a bent

She bettered those of Ypres and of Ghent.[19]

In all the parish not a dame dared stir

190　Towards the altar steps in front of her,

And if indeed they did, so wrath was she

As to be quite put out of charity.

Her kerchiefs were of finely woven ground;[20]

I dared have sworn they weighed a good ten pound,

195　The ones she wore on Sunday, on her head.

Her hose were of the finest scarlet red

And gartered tight; her shoes were soft and new.

Bold was her face, handsome, and red in hue.

A worthy woman all her life, what's more

200　She'd had five husbands, all at the church door,[21]

Apart from other company in youth;

No need just now to speak of that, forsooth.

And she had thrice been to Jerusalem,

Seen many strange rivers and passed over them;

205　She'd been to Rome and also to Boulogne,

St. James of Compostella and Cologne,

And she was skilled in wandering by the way.

She had gap-teeth, set widely, truth to say.

Easily on an ambling horse she sat

210　Well wimpled[22] up, and on her head a hat

As broad as is a buckler or a shield;

She had a flowing mantle that concealed

Large hips, her heels spurred sharply under that.

In company she liked to laugh and chat

---

19. Ypres (EE pruh) **and of Ghent:** Flemish centers of the wool trade.
20. ground: type of cloth.
21. church door: In Chaucer's day the marriage ceremony was performed at the church door.
22. wimpled: A wimple is a linen covering for the head and neck.

Your TURN

CHARACTERIZATION

In Chaucer's day, people approached the altar in order of their rank or status in society. In lines 189–192, what does the Wife of Bath's demand that she be first at the altar suggest about her character?

_____

_____

_____

_____

_____

_____

Your TURN

ANALYZING KEY DETAILS

What do the names of places in lines 203–207 tell you about the Wife of Bath?

_____

_____

_____

_____

_____

_____

_____

215 And knew the remedies for love's mischances,
   An art in which she knew the oldest dances.

IN OTHER WORDS   The Wife of Bath is quite a character. Her great pride is the fine cloth she weaves, and she considers herself the most important woman in her church. She has been married five times and has already been on three pilgrimages. A big, red-faced woman who wears an enormous hat and bright red stockings, she enjoys laughing and talking with the other pilgrims.

The Parson

A holy-minded man of good renown
There was, and poor, the *Parson* to a town,
Yet he was rich in holy thought and work.
220 He also was a learned man, a clerk,
Who truly knew Christ's gospel and would preach it
Devoutly to parishioners, and teach it.
Benign and wonderfully diligent,[23]
And patient when adversity was sent
225 (For so he proved in much adversity)
He hated cursing to extort a fee,
Nay rather he preferred beyond a doubt
Giving to poor parishioners round about
Both from church offerings and his property;
230 He could in little find sufficiency.
Wide was his parish, with houses far asunder,
Yet he neglected not in rain or thunder,
In sickness or in grief, to pay a call
On the remotest, whether great or small,
235 Upon his feet, and in his hand a stave.[24]

---

23. **diligent** (DIHL uh juhnt): careful and persistent in work.
24. **stave**: staff.

Your TURN

CHARACTERIZATION

Underline the words in lines 217–222 that the narrator uses to give direct characterization of the Parson.

Here's HOW

VOCABULARY

In line 224, it says that the Parson was patient "when adversity (ad VUR suh tee) was sent." After reading the rest of the section about the Parson, I think *adversity* must mean "hardship" or "suffering." I checked *adversity* in a dictionary, and that is the correct meaning.

This noble example to his sheep he gave
That first he wrought, and afterward he taught;
And it was from the Gospel he had caught
Those words, and he would add this figure too,
240 That if gold rust, what then will iron do?
For if a priest be foul in whom we trust
No wonder that a common man should rust;
And shame it is to see—let priests take stock—
A shitten shepherd and a snowy flock.
245 The true example that a priest should give
Is one of cleanness, how the sheep should live.
He did not set his benefice to hire[25]
And leave his sheep encumbered in the mire
Or run to London to earn easy bread
250 By singing masses for the wealthy dead,
Or find some Brotherhood and get enrolled.[26]
He stayed at home and watched over his fold
So that no wolf should make the sheep miscarry.
He was a shepherd and no mercenary.
255 Holy and virtuous he was, but then
Never contemptuous of sinful men,
Never disdainful, never too proud or fine,
But was discreet[27] in teaching and benign.
His business was to show a fair behavior
260 And draw men thus to Heaven and their Savior,
Unless indeed a man were obstinate;
And such, whether of high or low estate,
He put to sharp rebuke, to say the least.
I think there never was a better priest.
265 He sought no pomp or glory in his dealings,
No scrupulosity had spiced his feelings.
Christ and His Twelve Apostles and their lore
He taught, but followed it himself before.

---

25. **benefice to hire:** He did not hire someone else to perform his duties.
26. **find . . . enrolled:** He did not take a job as a paid chaplain to a guild.
27. **discreet** (dihs KREET): cautious about one's words or actions.

IN OTHER WORDS The Parson is very different from the Monk and the Nun. He takes his religion seriously, both in his studies and in the way he lives. Although poor himself, he gives generously to those in need. He goes on foot to visit the members of his parish even when he is ill or the weather is stormy. The Parson is kind and humble toward everyone. In short, he practices what he preaches, and he seeks to teach by his own example.

The Pardoner

H²⁸ and a gentle *Pardoner* rode together,

270 A bird from Charing Cross of the same feather,

Just back from visiting the Court of Rome.

He loudly sang *"Come hither, love, come home!"*

The Summoner sang deep seconds²⁹ to this song,

No trumpet ever sounded half so strong.

275 This Pardoner had hair as yellow as wax,

Hanging down smoothly like a hank of flax.

In driblets fell his locks behind his head

Down to his shoulders which they overspread;

Thinly they fell, like rat-tails, one by one.

280 He wore no hood upon his head, for fun;

The hood inside his wallet had been stowed,

He aimed at riding in the latest mode;

But for a little cap his head was bare

And he had bulging eye-balls, like a hare.

285 He'd sewed a holy relic on his cap;

His wallet lay before him on his lap,

Brimful of pardons³⁰ come from Rome, all hot.

Your
TURN

CHARACTERIZATION

In Chaucer's England, long hair was against the rules for men who worked for the church. These men had to wear their hair "tonsured"—short, with a shaved spot at the top, as a symbol of humility. Underline three other details in lines 275–284 that suggest that the Pardoner is not a holy man.

---

28. **He:** the Summoner.
29. **deep seconds:** harmonies.
30. **pardons:** small strips of parchment with papal seals attached. They were sold as indulgences (pardons for sins), with the proceeds supposedly going to a religious house. Many pardoners were dishonest, and even loyal church members often ridiculed them.

He had the same small voice a goat has got.

His chin no beard had harbored, nor would harbor,

290 Smoother than ever chin was left by barber.

I judge he was a gelding, or a mare.

As to his trade, from Berwick down to Ware

There was no pardoner of equal grace,

For in his trunk he had a pillow-case

295 Which he asserted was Our Lady's veil.

He said he had a gobbet[31] of the sail

Saint Peter had the time when he made bold

To walk the waves, till Jesu Christ took hold.

He had a cross of metal set with stones

300 And, in a glass, a rubble of pigs' bones.

And with these relics, any time he found

Some poor up-country parson to astound,

In one short day, in money down, he drew

More than the parson in a month or two,

305 And by his flatteries and prevarication

Made monkeys of the priest and congregation.

But still to do him justice first and last

In church he was a noble ecclesiast.[32]

How well he read a lesson or told a story!

310 But best of all he sang an Offertory,[33]

For well he knew that when that song was sung

He'd have to preach and tune his honey-tongue

And (well he could) win silver from the crowd.

That's why he sang so merrily and loud.

---

31. **gobbet:** fragment.
32. **ecclesiast** (ih KLEE zee ast): practitioner of church ritual.
33. **Offertory:** hymn sung while offerings are collected in church.

Characterization

Some people believe that Chaucer's pilgrims represent every type of human being. Pick one pilgrim, and describe how he or she is like at least three people you know or know of—you may compare the pilgrims with friends, relatives, or famous characters from movies or television.

The pilgrim I have chosen is: _____

1. A person or famous character who is like this pilgrim is: _____

I think the pilgrim and this person / character are alike because:

_____

_____

_____

_____

_____

_____

2. A person or famous character who is like this pilgrim is: _____

I think the pilgrim and this person / character are alike because:

_____

_____

_____

_____

_____

_____

3. A person or famous character who is like this pilgrim is: _____

I think the pilgrim and this person / character are alike because:

_____

_____

_____

_____

_____

Federigo's Falcon

Literary Focus: Situational Irony

Situational irony occurs when what actually happens in a story is the opposite of what we expect will happen. A good example is the story of King Midas from Greek mythology. Midas values riches above all else and wishes that everything he touched would turn to gold. His wish is granted, but Midas soon discovers that his touch turns food, drink, and even his beloved daughter to gold. Midas had expected his golden touch to make him happy; instead, it makes him miserable. Situational irony always produces an unexpected (and often unwelcome) result.

Reading Skill: Evaluating Historical Context

Historical context—the period in history in which a story is set— affects how the characters in the story act. In this medieval love story, pay attention to the ways the characters are like—and unlike— the characters in love stories today or even the people you know in real life. Keep in mind the characters you have seen in movies and TV shows, as well.

Into the Story

"Federigo's Falcon" is part of a collection of stories called the *Decameron.* Giovanni Boccaccio wrote them in fourteenth-century Italy soon after a terrible sickness struck the city of Florence. The stories are supposedly told by a group of wealthy young people who flee to a house in the country to escape the sickness. The young people decide that, for each of ten days (*decameron* is taken from the Greek words for "ten" and "day"), they will elect a king or queen. The king or queen will choose a theme that the others must use to tell a story. "Federigo's Falcon" is the ninth story told on the fifth day. This day was devoted to telling stories with happy endings.

from the **Decameron**

Federigo's Falcon

Giovanni Boccaccio

BASED ON THE TRANSLATION BY

Mark Musa and Peter Bondanella

EVALUATING THE HISTORICAL CONTEXT

In lines 1-9, there are several things that tell me that this story is set in medieval times. Federigo competes in tournaments, he is a knight, and he uses a spear. Also, I think that politeness and good manners may have been more important in that time.

SITUATIONAL IRONY

In lines 21-29, I would expect the poverty of Federigo to keep him far away from the rich Monna Giovanna. However, the opposite has happened: Federigo's poverty has brought him close to her, and Federigo's falcon is the one thing she needs.

VOCABULARY

I think the word *gravely* in line 26 means the same as *seriously*. I can substitute the word *seriously* for *gravely*, and the meaning of the sentence stays the same. That means these two words are *synonyms*—words that have the same meaning.

Once a young man named Federigo Alberighi[1] lived in the city of Florence, in what is now Italy. He was famous for his skill with weapons and also for his politeness and good manners. Federigo fell madly in love with a beautiful and charming married lady named
5 Monna Giovanna.

To win her love, he competed in jousts and tournaments—contests in which a knight on horseback carrying a long spear tries to knock an opponent off his horse. Federigo gave splendid feasts and spent his money extravagantly.

10 Monna Giovanna cared little for the things Federigo did to impress her, nor did she love him, but he loved her more than ever.

When he'd spent all his money, Federigo was forced to leave Florence; he went to live on his small farm near Campi, where he passed his time hawking whenever he could. His falcon, one of the
15 best in all the world, hunted birds and other small animals.

Now about this time, Monna Giovanna's very rich husband became ill and died. In his will, as was the law at that time, the husband left his fortune to their young son. However, he loved his wife dearly, so he stated in his will that if their son died without
20 having a son of his own, she would inherit everything.

The young widow and her son spent a year in the country, which was customary in those days after the death of a close relative. Her farm in Campi was very close to Federigo's farm, and her son and Federigo soon became friends. The boy began to enjoy working with
25 hunting dogs and birds of prey—especially Federigo's falcon.

One day the boy became gravely ill, and Monna Giovanni was much grieved, for she loved her only child enormously. She begged him to tell her if there was anything he desired. "I will do everything possible to get it for you," she vowed.

30 "Mother, if you can arrange for me to have Federigo's falcon, I think I would be well very soon," he told her.

---

1. Federigo Alberighi (FED uhr EE go AWL buh REE gee).

"Fifth Day, Ninth Story"(retitled "Federigo's Falcon") adapted from *The Decameron* by Giovanni Boccaccio, translated by Mark Musa and Peter Bondanella. Retold by Holt, Rinehart and Winston. Translation copyright © 1982 by Mark Musa and Peter Bondanella. Reproduced by permission of **W. W. Norton & Company, Inc**.

Monna Giovanna was taken aback and didn't know what to do. She knew that Federigo had loved her for many years although she'd never encouraged him. She thought, "How can I ask him for his

35 famous falcon, which is his only means of support and his only pleasure?"

She considered all this for a long time and finally told her son, "Think only of getting well, and tomorrow I shall bring you Federigo's falcon."

40 The next morning she and a companion walked to Federigo's modest house. When he heard that Monna Giovanna was asking for him at the door, Federigo was surprised and happy, and he welcomed her courteously.

"Greetings, Federigo!" she began. "I know that you have suffered

45 on my account by loving me more than you needed to, so I have come to repay you for the harm I've caused. My companion and I intend to dine with you today—just a simple meal."

Federigo humbly replied, "Madame, I don't remember having suffered any harm because of you; on the contrary, I have received

50 much good, and I am extremely happy to see you." He asked her to wait in his garden while he set the table.

Worried that he had nothing to serve her, he searched his house for money or for something to pawn to buy food, but he found nothing. Then, he spied his good falcon, perched in a small room.

55 This, he thought, is worthy food for such a lady. He wrung the plump bird's neck and had a servant prepare and roast it on a spit.

He set the table with the whitest of tablecloths and called the two women to lunch. They never dreamed that they were eating the falcon.

60 After lunch, Monna Giovanni told Federigo, "You will be amazed when you hear why I came. I wish you had a child of your own that you loved because then I'm certain you would forgive me, at least partly. The common laws of motherhood force me—against my will and against good manners—to ask you for a gift—for your most

65 precious possession—your falcon. I fear that my son, who lies very ill, may die if I don't bring it to him. I ask you not because of your love for me, but because of your own nobility."

VOCABULARY

The word *support* in line 35 can mean "to keep from falling" or "to provide for." Which meaning do you think it has here? Explain your answer.

_____

_____

_____

EVALUATING THE HISTORICAL CONTEXT

In lines 44–51, does the language used by Monna Giovanna and Federigo show that this story is not happening today? Explain your answer.

_____

_____

_____

_____

SITUATIONAL IRONY

In lines 54–59, what is the situational irony in Federigo's decision to kill his falcon and serve it for dinner?

_____

_____

_____

Here's HOW

EVALUATING THE HISTORICAL CONTEXT

It seems that women in the time of this story were not free to marry anyone they pleased. In lines 85-89, Monna Giovanna has to get her brothers' approval to marry.

Your TURN

SITUATIONAL IRONY

Irony is not always sad; sometimes, the ironic twist can be a happy one. Read lines 85–98, and tell how this happy situation is ironic.

_____

_____

_____

_____

_____

_____

_____

_____

_____

_____

_____

_____

Then, Federigo wept bitterly in her presence. He knew he couldn't grant her request, for she had just eaten the falcon. He wept and
70 could not utter a word.

At first she thought he was crying because he was sad to lose his falcon. She almost withdrew her request, but she held back and waited for his reply.

"My lady," he said finally, "ever since first I loved you, Fortune
75 has been cruel to me, but nothing compares to what she has just done to me; I will never be at peace with her again. I judged my falcon to be a food worthy of you, so I had it roasted and served to you."

As proof, he laid the falcon's feathers, feet, and beak before her.
80 Monna Giovanna scolded him for killing so fine a falcon to serve as a meal to a woman, but she also realized that Federigo had a greatness of spirit that his poverty would never diminish.

She thanked Federigo for the honor he had paid her and for his good will. To her immense sorrow, her son died a few days later.
85 When her period of mourning ended, her brothers urged her to remarry, for she was very rich and still young. She did not want to remarry, but she began to think of Federigo's generosity, so she told her brothers, "I'd really prefer to remain a widow. But if you insist that I marry, the only man I'll consider marrying is Federigo."
90 "You foolish woman," her brothers laughed at her, "how can you want a man who hasn't a penny to his name?"

"I know that," she replied, "but I would rather have a man who needs money than money that needs a man."

Her brothers soon realized that she was determined, and although
95 Federigo was poor, he was of noble birth. So Federigo and the very rich widow, Monna Giovanni, were married. He managed their financial affairs carefully, and they lived happily together for the rest of his days.

Plot

The **plot** is the series of related events that make up a story. The plot is a story's underlying structure. Most plots contain the elements listed below:

The **exposition** presents the characters, the setting, and necessary background information.

The **conflict** is a struggle or clash between opposing characters, forces, or emotions.

Complications are further developments that intensify the main conflict.

The **climax** is the most exciting part of the plot, where something happens to determine the outcome of the conflict.

The **resolution** is the unraveling of all the problems or mysteries of the plot.

In the space below, list details from "Federigo's Falcon" that correspond to the five principal elements of plot. **Exposition** and **Complications** have been done for you.

Exposition The main characters are Federigo Alberighi and Monna Giovanna. The setting is Florence. Federigo loves Monna. He tries to win her love by being a knight, and he spends all his money.
Conflict
Complications The death of Monna's husband; the move to the country, close to Federigo's farm; the boy's love for the falcon; the boy's illness and request.
Climax
Resolution

The Renaissance 1485–1660

The term *renaissance* (REHN uh sahns) is a French word meaning
"rebirth." In history it refers to the period of time following the
Middle Ages. During the Middle Ages, <u>the writings of ancient Greece
and Rome</u> had been forgotten. During the Renaissance, people
5 rediscovered the marvels of the Greek and Latin classics. People
became more curious about themselves and the world. They began
creating beautiful things and thinking new, daring thoughts. The
human spirit itself was reborn.

It All Began in Italy

10 The Renaissance began in Italy in the 1300s. There, much wealth had
been gained through trade with the East and banking. This wealth led
to an interest in art, the world, and the planets and stars. Artists such
as Michelangelo, explorers such as Columbus, and scientists such as
Galileo all lived and worked during the Italian Renaissance.

15   Wealthy and powerful, the Roman Catholic Church supported
many Renaissance artists and thinkers. Pope Julian II, for example,
hired Michelangelo to paint scenes from the Bible on the ceiling of the
Sistine Chapel. The figures in these scenes are bright, heroic, and
noble. Many Renaissance artists shared Michelangelo's hopeful view
20 of humanity.

Humanism: Questions About the Good Life

The Renaissance writers were part of a movement known as
humanism (HYOO muh nihz uhm). They read the forgotten Latin and
Greek classics to discover new answers to such questions as "What
25 is a human being?" and "What is a good life?" Christianity already
provided answers to these questions. The humanists accepted these
answers but hoped to find support for them in the ancient texts.

     The humanists had two tasks. First, they needed to find true
copies that were the same as the original ancient writings. Their
30 searches through monasteries uncovered many long-forgotten texts.
Next, they needed to share their findings. They set up universities and
became teachers of the young men who, they hoped, would be the
world's next leaders.

Here's HOW

VOCABULARY

I think the word *classics* in line 5 means "the writings of ancient Greece and Rome." I have underlined these words in lines 3–4.

Here's HOW

VOCABULARY

I know that the word *tasks* in line 28 means the same as *jobs*. That means that *tasks* and *jobs* are synonyms.

The New Technology: A Flood of Print

35 Around 1455, a German named Johannes Gutenberg[1] printed the first complete book, a huge Bible in Latin. Before this, books had been written by hand. Now, books could be produced faster and more cheaply. Gutenberg's printing press made more information available to many more people.

40 Printing came to England in 1476, when a merchant named William Caxton set up a printing press near London. His press started the flood of print in English that continues today.

Two Friends—Two Humanists

A Dutch monk named Desiderius Erasmus is perhaps the best known 45 of all the Renaissance humanists. Erasmus traveled widely, often visiting England to teach Greek at Cambridge University. While there, he became close friends with Thomas More.

More was a lawyer and also a writer. Like Erasmus, he wrote in Latin. He produced poems, pamphlets, and biographies, as well as his 50 most famous work, *Utopia* (1516). This work, which describes an imaginary society, became popular overnight. It has been translated into many languages and is often imitated. In addition, it has given us an adjective to describe idealized social systems: *utopian*.

The Reformation: Breaking with the Church

55 While the Renaissance was going on throughout Europe, another important event, the Reformation, was taking place in some countries. One feature of the Reformation was the same in all countries—the authority of the pope was rejected.

In England, conflicts with the Roman Catholic Church had been 60 going on for centuries. By the 1530s, though, a break with Rome became unavoidable. Strong feelings of patriotism made the English resent the power of the far-off pope. Moreover, new ideas about religion were coming into England from other countries, especially Germany. There, a monk named Martin Luther had started a new 65 form of Christianity. It was based not on what the pope said, but on

VOCABULARY

The word *press* can mean "to smooth clothing with a hot iron," "newspapers, magazines, news services," or "a machine that prints out newspapers, books, or magazines." Which meaning do you think it has in line 41? Explain your answer.

_____

_____

_____

VOCABULARY

The word *flood* in line 42 can mean "a great supply" or "an overflowing of water." Which meaning do you think it has in this line? Why?

_____

_____

_____

VOCABULARY

I know that the word *reform* means "make better." *Reform* is in the large word *Reformation* in line 56. I think the people who were part of the Reformation wanted to make the church better.

---

1. **Johannes Gutenberg** (yoh HAHN uhs GOOT uhn BUHRG).

a person's own understanding of the Bible. In England, humanists like Thomas More began challenging the old ways of the Roman Church. The Catholic Church's superstitions, its immoral clergy, and its wealth, More said, all needed to be reformed.

King Versus Pope

70 King Henry VIII had a problem: He wanted to get rid of his wife, Catherine of Aragon. Married for twenty-four years, Henry and Catherine of Aragon had not had a son who could inherit Henry's throne. In addition, a younger woman, Anne Boleyn, had become the

75 king's "favorite." But the Church did not allow divorce.

Henry asked Pope Clement VII to declare that he and Catherine had never been properly married. When his request was denied in 1533, Henry declared himself the head of the English Church. He named a new archbishop of Canterbury, who declared Henry's

80 marriage to Catherine legally over. Protestantism in England had begun.

Henry closed all of England's monasteries and sold their land to his subjects. Some of his subjects, though, remained loyal to the pope. Sir Thomas More—now a knight and Lord Chancellor of England—

85 was one of them. For his disloyalty to Henry, the king had More beheaded.

Other people were dissatisfied with the new church for different reasons: They felt that it was not reformed *enough*. These people, known as Puritans, wanted to purify the church of all its outward

90 "extras"—bishops, prayer books, even stained-glass windows. They saw religion as an inward, private matter between a person and God.

Henry VIII: Rule by the Sword

Henry VIII was the second of five Tudor kings. (His father, Henry VII, had seized the throne at the end of a long struggle called the Wars of

95 the Roses.) During his reign, Henry VIII had six wives. These were Catherine of Aragon, Anne Boleyn, Jane Seymour, Anne of Cleves,

Here's HOW

VOCABULARY

I think the word *Protestantism* in line 80 is the name of the new church that King Henry started in England. The smaller word *protest*, which means "to act against," is in the large word *Protestantism*. Henry was protesting against the pope. Also, *Protestantism* begins with a capital letter, which means it is the name of something.

Your TURN

VOCABULARY

What is the meaning of *subjects* in line 83? Give at least one other meaning of the word *subjects*.

_____

_____

_____

_____

_____

_____

_____

Catherine Howard, and Catherine Parr. The fates of these women can be summarized in this rhyme:

Divorced, beheaded, died,

100   Divorced, beheaded, survived.

Henry was unfaithful to his wives, but he couldn't bear the thought that they might be unfaithful to him. Anne Boleyn and Catherine Howard paid the price of Henry's suspicions by being beheaded.

Despite his troubled home life, Henry VIII was an important king.
105 He created the Royal Navy, which increased England's power all over the globe. He supported humanistic learning. He wrote poetry, played musical instruments, and was a superb athlete. As an old man, he was bossy and self-centered. He died not knowing that his daughter would become the greatest ruler England ever had.

110 ## The Boy King and Bloody Mary

Henry VIII had three children: Mary, daughter of Catherine of Aragon; Elizabeth, daughter of Anne Boleyn; and Edward, son of Jane Seymour. Because he was the only male, Edward was first in line for the throne. Crowned Edward VI in 1547, at the age of nine, the sickly
115 boy was a ruler in name only.

When Edward died, in 1553, his half sister Mary took the throne. Mary, a devout Catholic, was angry with her father for murdering her mother. In a fit of revenge, she restored the Catholic Church in England. She hunted down Protestants and burned many of them at
120 the stake. She also married the king of Spain, a country England was beginning to fear. These actions, among others, earned her the hatred of many of her subjects. When "Bloody Mary" died childless, in 1558, her half-sister, Elizabeth, became queen.

Elizabeth: The Virgin Queen

125 Elizabeth I (reigned 1558–1603) was one of the most brilliant rulers in history. Her first task was to bring back order in a country torn apart by religious feuds. She again declared the Church of England separate from the Roman Catholic Church. To keep Spain happy, she hinted that, now that Mary was dead, she might marry Mary's
130 widower, King Philip II.

VOCABULARY

What might be a synonym— a word that means the same thing—for *feuds* in line 127? Be sure your synonym can be substituted for *feuds* and still keep the same meaning for that sentence.

_____

_____

_____

Philip was the first of many noblemen who wanted to marry Elizabeth. But this "Virgin Queen" (after whom our state of Virginia was named) refused to marry anyone. She knew that her strength lay in her independence—in her ability to promise marriage but to remain
135 forever single.

A truly heroic person, Elizabeth survived many plots against her life. Many of these plots were the work of Elizabeth's cousin Mary, Queen of Scots (in Scotland). This Mary was a descendent of Henry VII and next in line to the English throne. A Catholic, she was
140 eventually removed from power in Protestant Scotland. She lived for many years under house arrest in England. Finally, Elizabeth had her executed.

The Defeat of the Spanish Armada

Elizabeth rejected King Philip of Spain as a husband. In 1588, Philip
145 was fed up and sent a huge fleet of warships—an armada—to attack England. With the help of some nasty weather, England's Royal Navy destroyed the Armada. This victory set England firmly apart from the Catholic nations of Europe. It was a great turning point in history and probably Elizabeth's finest moment.

150 ## A Flood of Literature

Now firmly sure of themselves, the English started writing as never before. Elizabeth became a much-loved symbol of peace and security. She inspired English authors, many of whom wrote about her in their poetry, drama, and fiction. Other writers honored this learned queen
155 by dedicating their works to her.

The Glass of Fashion: Renaissance Clothing

Simply put, Renaissance styles in clothing for the noble and wealthy were extreme. Every morning, men strolled up and down the center aisle of St. Paul's Church to show off their finery. They loved rich
160 fabrics, silk stockings, and platform shoes. They wore earrings, bracelets, and sometimes makeup.

In the 1580s and 1590s, clothes were used to exaggerate the human form. Starched neck ruffs stretched from shoulder to shoulder.

Women's hoop skirts could be four feet wide at the hips, and men's full, thigh-length pants were padded. Stockings made a man's knees and calves look more shapely.

Braids, bows, and lace covered most garments. Colors were rich and bold; red, gold, black, and white were favorites. Colors and flowers also had symbolic meanings. Green meant love, for example, and a pansy stood for sadness. Queen Elizabeth often wore white and black together—colors that symbolized purity.

Decline of the Renaissance

When Elizabeth died childless, James VI of Scotland came to the throne. (James was the son of Mary, Queen of Scots.) As James I of England (reigned 1603–1625), he lacked Elizabeth's skill and grace. James spent where Elizabeth had saved; he spoke poorly where she had been eloquent. He was a foreigner, while she had been a true Englishwoman.

James I tried hard. He wrote books, supported Shakespeare, and ordered a new translation of the Bible. He was a generous and peaceful ruler. But many of his subjects—especially the Puritans—greatly disliked his style.

His son, Charles I (reigned 1625–1649), had an even worse time as king. His stubborn ways earned him many enemies, and he was beheaded in 1649. For eleven years, England was ruled by Parliament and the Puritan dictator Oliver Cromwell.

When Charles's son was returned to the throne in 1660, England had changed. Renaissance energies gradually gave out. Educated people were becoming more worldly in their outlook. New scientific truths were beginning to challenge long-standing religious beliefs.

Major Characteristics of the Renaissance

- People rediscovered ancient Greek and Roman writers.
- Humanism focused on how to live a good, virtuous life.
- Printing made books more widely available.
- A growing merchant class challenged the power of the Church.
- The spread of scholarly Latin made possible the sharing of ideas.

VOCABULARY

The word *eloquent* in line 177 is defined in the text using a phrase that has the opposite meaning. Underline the phrase. What does *eloquent* mean?

_____

_____

_____

VOCABULARY

What is the meaning of *dictator* in line 186? What word in the same sentence helps you figure out this meaning?

_____

_____

_____

_____

_____

Meditation 17

Literary Focus: Tone

Tone is the attitude a writer takes toward the reader, the subject, or a character in a literary work. For example, one writer may express a positive attitude on the subject of love, and another writer may express a negative attitude. Writers convey their tones through the words, images, and details they choose. In Meditation 17, John Donne's tone supports his sad message.

Reading Skill: Using Context Clues

Context clues are the hints about meaning that you get from other words or phrases around an unfamiliar word. In Donne's meditation, for example, you may not know exactly what the word *toll* means. However, you will be able to make a good guess after reading the first sentence. It is a good idea to check your guesses on word meanings in a dictionary.

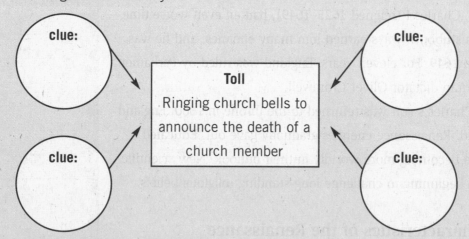

clue:

clue:

Toll
Ringing church bells to announce the death of a church member

clue:

clue:

Into the Meditation

Later in his life, when he was very ill, Donne wrote several meditations on death and dying, one of which is "Meditation 17."

Meditation 17

BASED ON THE MEDITATION BY
John Donne

Meditation 17

Nunc lento	Now, this bell tolling softly
sonitu dicunt,	for another, says to me,
Morieris.	Thou must die.

CONTEXT CLUES

In line 6 of Meditation 17, draw a circle around the word *toll*. Then, re-read lines 1–6, and draw lines under the words that help you understand the meaning of *toll*. You might like to put these words in the graphic organizer on page 56.

TONE

In lines 10-15, Donne says that people are all part of a book written by God. He goes on to say people are translated, just as books are translated from one language to another. He also says that God will gather the people together in heaven, like pages in a book. Donne's tone is very serious and matter-of-fact. He doesn't use emotional language.

Perhaps the person for whom this death bell tolls is so ill that he
5 does not know it rings for him. Maybe I think that I am all right; but
those around me see my actual state, and toll the death bell for me.
The church is universal, and so is everything that happens in the
church. When a child is baptized, we are linked together because
both of us are now connected to the Head of the church—to Christ.
10 In the same way I am affected by every death: We are all part of
one book written by God. When one person dies, a chapter is not
torn out of the book. He or she is translated, that is, moved into the
afterlife by one of God's many translators—age, sickness and war, or
justice. God both oversees the translation and rebinds the pages for
15 the final opening in the Library, which is heaven. Just as the bell
rings to call both the preacher and the congregation to the church
service, so the death bell tolls for all of us—but especially for me,
because I am very ill and near death. There was once an argument
that went as far as a lawsuit as to which religious order should ring
20 the bell that calls us to prayer in the morning. It was decided that the
first one to awaken in the morning would ring the bell. And so it is
with the death bell—we should awake early to the fact that the bell
tolls for us as well as the person who is dying. No one can ignore
the tolling of this bell—it connects us all to one another and to death.
25 No one person is an island, alone and unconnected. Every human is
like a piece of a continent, a part of a mainland. If one small lump of
dirt is washed away from this mainland, it is smaller—it is
diminished. If one person dies, it is like that clump of earth being
washed away from the mainland—all of us are affected, all of us are

30 diminished. Therefore, you should never ask for whom the death bell

is ringing; it tolls for you and for me. Every one of us must die, and

another's death reminds us of our own death to come. We cannot call

this a borrowing of misery and pain, as if we did not have enough

misfortune of our own and had to get it from someone else. That

35 would be like wanting someone else's treasure. Misfortune, pain, and

trouble are all a treasure—no one has enough of it. This treasure

helps us get nearer to God. Like money, great trouble and misfortune

have little worth when they are stored away out of sight. However,

misery and misfortune are valuable when they are used to help others

40 turn to God. We must welcome suffering because it helps us get to

Heaven.

Your
TURN

VOCABULARY

Donne uses the word *treasure* in line 35. Draw a line under the words that, according to the author, make up this treasure. Look for these words in lines 30–41.

Tone

A writer reveals his or her attitude toward the reader, a subject, or a character through the **tone** that he or she has. Tone is conveyed through the writer's choice of words and details. What is the tone of Meditation 17? Does its tone remain constant throughout, or does it change? In this chart, state briefly what tone or tones you can find in Meditation 17, and then jot down the words, details, or figures of speech that Donne uses to convey this tone.

Tone	Words/Details
1.	
2.	

Vocabulary Development

Word Maps: Pinning Down Word Meanings

Word Bank
diminished
misery
misfortune
treasure

A **word map** can help you to clarify all the ways a word can be used. Study this sample word map for the word *misery*. Then, with a partner, make a word map for each of the other words in the Word Bank. (You will need to make up some of your own questions.) Exchange your word maps with other teams. Can they think of new questions to ask about a word?

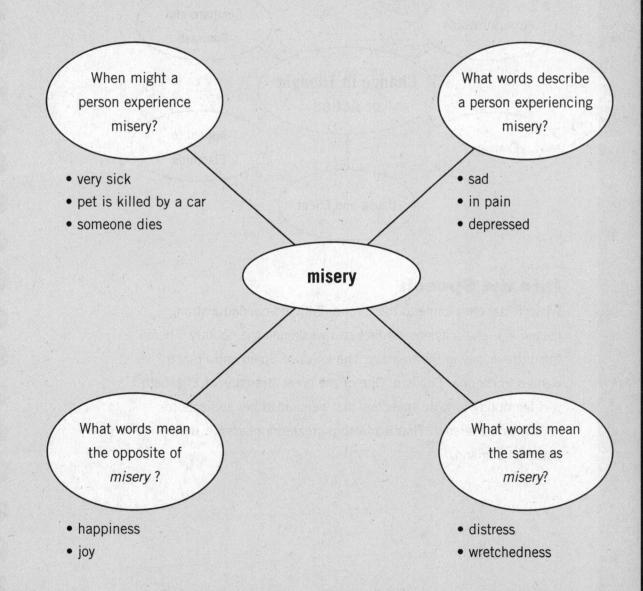

When might a person experience misery?
- very sick
- pet is killed by a car
- someone dies

What words describe a person experiencing misery?
- sad
- in pain
- depressed

misery

What words mean the opposite of *misery*?
- happiness
- joy

What words mean the same as *misery*?
- distress
- wretchedness

Tilbury Speech

Reading Skill: Understanding Persuasion

Persuasive speakers focus on a particular subject, main idea, or point of view. The main aim of persuasive speakers is to change the way their listeners think or to get their listeners to carry out an action.

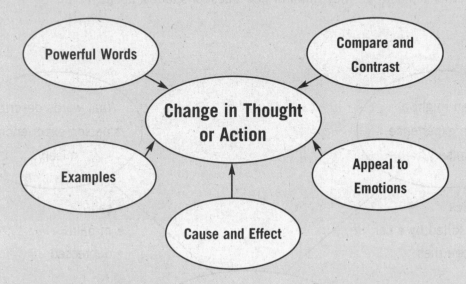

Into the Speech

When Elizabeth I came to the throne, England needed a strong leader. War and religious conflict had weakened the country. There was little money in the treasury. The kings of Spain and France wanted to conquer England. One of the great strengths of Elizabeth I was her ability to write speeches that persuaded her subjects to follow her leadership. That leadership created a peaceful, rich, and powerful England.

Tilbury Speech

BASED ON THE SPEECH BY

Elizabeth I

Here's
HOW

UNDERSTANDING PERSUASIVE TECHNIQUES

In lines 1–8, Elizabeth uses the phrase "my loving people" three times. I think that repeating this phrase so many times reminds her people that they do love their powerful queen.

Your
TURN

UNDERSTANDING PERSUASIVE TECHNIQUES

Who does Elizabeth compare herself with in lines 12–14? What is she saying about herself when she makes this comparison?

_____

_____

_____

_____

_____

_____

_____

_____

_____

_____

_____

_____

_____

YOU NEED TO KNOW Queen Elizabeth I wrote powerful speeches and political addresses. One of her best-known speeches is the "Tilbury Speech." Queen Elizabeth gave this speech in 1588. The news that the Spanish Armada had been destroyed had not yet reached England, and Elizabeth believed the Spanish were on their way to invade England. She wanted to inspire her army to defend England against the Spaniards. In this speech the English queen shows her deep feeling for—and pride in—her people and her nation.

My loving people: Some have tried to persuade me that it is dangerous to give you arms and ammunition. They warn that armed people might turn on me and attack me. But I assure you I do not want to live distrusting my faithful and loving people. Let tyrants—

5 those who are cruel and absolute rulers—fear to arm their people. I have always behaved myself so that, under God, I can place my greatest strength and safeguard in the loyal hearts and goodwill of my subjects—my loving people. Therefore I am here with you, as you can see, not to amuse myself, but determined to be with you in the heat

10 of the battle. I am here to live or die with you. I will die for my God, and for my kingdom, and for my people. I will let my honor and my blood be brought down in the dust. I know I have the body of a weak and feeble woman, but I have the heart and courage of a king—and of a king of England, too. I do not think that Parma, or Spain, or any

15 prince of Europe should dare to invade the borders of my kingdom. So, not wanting to be a shameful coward, I myself will take up arms. I myself will be your general and your judge. I will be the person who rewards every one of you for your courage in the field of battle. I know that you already deserve rewards and crowns for your courage,

20 and I do assure you, on the word of a prince, they shall be duly paid to you.

Persuasion

Persuasion is a type of writing or speaking designed to change the way a reader or listener thinks or acts. Persuasive writing can be found in speeches, newspaper editorials, essays, articles, and advertisements.

Explain how each element or detail shown on the left-hand side of the chart below contributes to the queen's persuasive purpose in the "Tilbury Speech." The first one has been done for you.

Elements/Details	Persuasive Function
1. repetition of the words "loving people"	1. Powerful words are used to get the people to fight the enemy along with Elizabeth.
2. contrast with tyrants	2.
3. willingness to sacrifice life	3.
4. contrast between body of a woman and heart of a king	4.
5. assurance of "rewards and crowns"	5.

The Parable of the Prodigal Son

Literary Focus: Parable

A **parable** is a brief story that teaches a moral lesson about life. Parables convey their lessons through the use of **allegory**: The characters, places, and events in the story stand for broader, more complex ideas. The parables in the Christian scriptures draw their lessons from characters and situations that would have been familiar to people of Jesus' time.

Reading Skill: Summarizing

A **summary** is a short restatement of the main events and important ideas in a piece of literature. When you summarize a work, briefly identify the major characters. Then, in your own words, describe the characters' problems, state the main events, and explain how the problems are finally resolved. Remember to keep your summary simple, and leave out minor details.

Into the Parable

In ancient Israel—Jesus' homeland—the oldest son in a family would inherit a double share of his father's wealth and become the head of the family when his father died. In this parable the older son is about to inherit two thirds of his father's estate and the younger son is about to inherit one third. This would have been a common situation in Jesus' time. While a father was alive, he was not required to give any part of his estate to his sons.

The Parable of the Prodigal Son

BASED ON THE PARABLE FROM THE

King James Bible

There was once a man who had two sons, and the younger said to his father, "Father, give me my share of the property." A few days later the younger son sold his share, took the cash, and left home for a far-off country, where he wasted it all.

25   A famine came into that country. Food became scarce, and the young man could not feed himself. So he went to work for a farmer, who sent him to tend the pigs. He would have been glad to eat the slops that the pigs ate, but no one gave him anything. Then he thought, "My father's servants have more food than they can eat, while I am starving! I will go to my father and say to him, 'Father, I am no longer good enough to be called your son. Treat me like one of your servants.'"

So he started out for his father's house. As soon as his father saw him, he was overjoyed. He had thought his younger son was dead.

The father sent his servants for his best clothes to dress his son in, and he told them to prepare a feast to celebrate his son's return.

The older son was on his way back from the farm fields. As he came close to the house, he heard music and dancing. He asked one of the servants what was going on. The servant told him they were celebrating the younger brother's safe return.

The older son was angry and refused to go in, even though his father came out and begged him. He said that his father had never even given him a goat for a feast with his friends, and now they had killed the fat calf for his good-for-nothing brother.

"My boy," said the father, "you are always with me, and everything I have is yours. How could we not celebrate this happy day? Your brother here was dead, and now he has come back to life. He was lost, and now he is found."

Parable

A **parable** is a brief story that teaches a moral lesson about life. Parables convey these lessons through the use of **allegory**—a story with a message that can be understood on both a literal, surface level and a deeper level. The characters, objects, and events in parables stand for broader concepts.

In the chart below, the three characters from "The Parable of the Prodigal Son" are listed. Identify the broader concepts that these characters represent. Hints have been provided for each one.

Character	Hint	Broader Concept
1. father	The father represents a figure who is very generous and accepting.	
2. younger son	The younger son represents people who have behaved badly but are sorry for what they've done.	
3. older son	The older son represents a human quality that people feel when they want what other people have.	

The Restoration and the Eighteenth Century 1660–1800

During the 1600s, England had suffered many hardships: civil war, the plague, and a devastating fire in London. After such chaos the nation wanted peace and order. By the mid-1700s, these goals had largely been achieved. New English settlements were being set up
5 around the globe. The middle class was growing. The upper classes prospered. Thinkers and artists produced brilliant works and asked fascinating new questions.

Augustan and Neoclassical: Comparisons with Rome

England during this period is often compared with ancient Rome
10 during the reign of the emperor Augustus (63 B.C.–A.D. 14). Augustus brought peace and order to Rome after the previous emperor, Julius Caesar, was killed. Similarly, Charles II returned to the throne in England, and the monarchy was restored. Peace returned to England after the civil wars and the beheading of Charles I. Like the people of
15 ancient Rome, the people of England were tired of war, suspicious of radicals, and ready to settle down to the good life.

In this age the Latin classics were regarded as the best literary works. They were thought to represent what was universal in human experience. Therefore, many English writers modeled their works on
20 ancient Latin ones. Such writings were called *neoclassical*—"new classical."

Reason and Enlightenment: Asking "How"

This period is often referred to as the Age of Reason or the Enlightenment. These labels tell how people were gradually changing
25 their view of themselves and the world. In earlier ages, world events such as earthquakes and comets were seen as punishments or warnings. As the Enlightenment began, people started looking for scientific explanations of natural events.

For example, the astronomer Edmond Halley took the terror out of
30 comets appearing in the sky. He used math to calculate the length of
one comet's orbit: seventy-six years. He was then able to predict that
the comet would appear in 1786, 1834, 1919, and 1986—and it did.
Such a reasonable explanation showed that there was no connection
between the comet and human events. Seen in this way, natural
35 events became much less frightening, and superstitions began to fade.

Changes in Religion: More Questions

The new scientific explanations of nature began to affect some
people's religious views. If comets weren't warnings from God, maybe
God didn't meddle in human affairs at all. Perhaps the universe was
40 like a giant clock, set in motion by a Creator who then sat back and
watched it run on its own. This view was part of a larger movement
known as Deism (DEE ihz uhm). Some people worried that Deism
would make human beings lazy and self-satisfied. If the universe were
a machine, wouldn't it run regardless of what human beings did or
45 didn't do?

Although ideas about God were changing, few people dismissed
religion altogether. Great thinkers like Sir Isaac Newton and John
Locke remained religious. As it had in ages past, Christianity
continued to play a central role in most English people's lives.

50 ## Religion and Politics

When Charles II came to the throne, he again declared the Anglican
Church the official state church. (In the United States, the Anglican
Church is called the Episcopal Church.) Furthermore, he tried to
outlaw all church groups that were not Anglican, including the
55 Puritans. These groups were persecuted throughout the 1700s.

The Bloodless Revolution

When Charles II died, in 1685, his brother James II succeeded him.
James was a Roman Catholic, and most people in England deeply
distrusted him. After all, it was widely believed that Catholics were
60 plotting to hand the country over to the pope! Opposition to the king,

VOCABULARY

What do you think the word
calculate means in line 30?
Explain your answer.

_____

_____

_____

_____

_____

his queen, and their son became very intense. Finally, in 1688, the family fled to France. After this Glorious (bloodless) Revolution, the throne went to James's Protestant daughter, Mary, and her Dutch husband, William of Orange. The rulers of England have been
65 Anglicans ever since.

Addicted to the Theater

From 1642 to 1660, all theaters in England had been closed by Cromwell and the Puritans. But Charles II, who lived in France at the time, had become addicted to theatergoing. Once on the English
70 throne, he quickly repealed the ban on drama. A new excitement about theater rapidly spread. Now female roles could be played by women—not by men and boys as before. Many great comedies were produced during this period, including William Congreve's *The Way of the World*. These plays reflected the life of the pleasure-loving upper
75 classes. They also poked fun at this lifestyle, often showing the unromantic side of love and relationships.

Pope and Swift: Attacks on Bad Taste

Alexander Pope and Jonathan Swift are now considered the best writers of the early 1700s. At the time, though, both were out of step
80 with the values of the age—values that they criticized harshly. Many English people felt smug and satisfied with the world. Pope and Swift did not. They were horrified by the sloppiness they saw in art, manners, and morals. Pope, who loved order and discipline, attacked members of the upper classes for their bad behavior and bad taste.
85 Swift, too, aimed to expose the worst of human nature—much like the artist William Hogarth, whose paintings showed the sordid underside of life.

Journalism: A New Profession

While Swift and Pope focused on the upper classes, a writer named
90 Daniel Defoe stood for middle-class values: thrift, hard work, and responsibility. Defoe and other writers were developing a new form of professional writing—journalism. These first journalists did not merely

describe the events of the day. They also viewed themselves as
reformers: What they wrote could change society. Some journalists
95 today still see themselves in this role.

Public Poetry

Today many people think true poetry should reveal a poet's
innermost feelings—his or her soul. But the eighteenth-century
poets had no interest in exposing their souls. For them, poetry was
100 a product of their "wit," or their minds. It was a public rather than a
private expression.

These poets would decide ahead of time to make a particular kind
of poem, much as a carpenter decides to make a certain kind of chair.
Many of these poetic forms came from the classics.

105 For example, if an important person died, the poets would
celebrate that person by writing **elegies.** Such poems did not
necessarily tell the truth about a person. Instead, they said the very
best things that the poet could think of saying. On the other hand, if
the poets felt that a person was behaving badly, they might write a
110 **satire.** These poems did not tell the full truth about a person, either.
They made fun of the person's weaknesses.

Another important kind of poem was the **ode.** Like the satire and
the elegy, the ode used plenty of exaggeration. In lofty poetic
language, odes expressed the feelings of society at large. An ode might
115 be written, for instance, to celebrate the winning of a battle.

Like the fashions of the day, poems were carefully put together. To
go out in public, a person was expected to put on fancy, formal
clothes. Similarly, a poem was expected to be "dressed" in perfect
rhythms and rhymes. In no way was the Age of Reason a casual one.

120 The First English Novelists

By the mid-1700s, people were writing and reading long stories called
novels. (The word *novel* means "something new.") Middle-class
women particularly enjoyed these novels. They told of unlucky people
and their rambling, comical adventures.

VOCABULARY

What did Defoe think he could
do as a reformer (line 94)?

_____

_____

_____

_____

_____

_____

_____

VOCABULARY

In lines 121–124, underline
the words or phrases that
describe what appeared in the
long stories that were first
called *novels*.

125　　The most important novelist of the 1700s was Henry Fielding. His novels are crammed with rowdy incidents and characters who are good but not perfect. Other novelists such as Samuel Richardson and Laurence Sterne experimented with this new form. Richardson was the first to look closely at a character's emotions, while Sterne used

130　the novel to challenge all the old "rules" of writing.

Living Conditions Among the Rich and the Poor

Life Among the "Haves." The wealthy enjoyed great luxury during this age. They divided their time between London and the country, dancing, dining, drinking, and gambling. They gathered at

135　coffeehouses and in the city's gardens to gossip, to see, and to be seen. Men wore velvet or satin coats, silk breeches, high-heeled shoes, and broad hats with feathers. They also wore pigtails and hair bows. Women wore low-cut silk dresses, enormous hoop skirts, and towering wigs—some reaching two or three feet in height!

140　**Life Among the "Have-Nots."** The poor, meanwhile, suffered great miseries. Overcrowding reached an all-time high in London tenements. An entire family might share a single, rat-infested room. Garbage and human waste were tossed into the streets. During the early 1700s, more people died than were born. In the worst years,

145　three out of every four children in London died before they reached age five. If they lived, they were often forced to work as soon as they were able.

Searching for a Simpler Life

By the 1780s, the world was changing. Factories were turning cities

150　into filthy slums. Across the English Channel the French were about to murder a king and drastically change their society. The age of elegance seemed to be ending.

　　Writers, too, were turning in new directions. Disgusted with the cities, they looked elsewhere for inspiration—to nature, to the

155　imagination, to the lives of simple country people, and to the past. A new literary age was quietly dawning.

Major Events of the Restoration and the Eighteenth Century

- With King Charles II came a period of peace and stability.
- Writers wrote in a "new classical" style based on the Greek and Latin classics.
- Scientists gave logical explanations for natural events. These explanations changed some people's religious views.
- Writers aimed to expose the moral corruption of society.
- Journalists commented on public manners and values.
- Novelists wrote long works of fiction to satisfy middle-class tastes.
- Theatergoing enjoyed a surge in popularity.
- At the end of the age, people began to crave the simplicity of nature.

A Modest Proposal

Literary Focus: Verbal Irony

Verbal irony occurs when a writer or a speaker says one thing but really means something quite different—usually the direct opposite. Let's say you have the flu and someone asks, "How are you?" Your response— "Great!"—spoken in a sarcastic tone, makes your irony clear.

Reading Skill: Recognizing Persuasive Techniques

One purpose of writing is to persuade. For example, politicians and advertisers want to convince the reader or listener of a certain point of view. To do this, they use certain techniques, or appeals. A **logical appeal** uses evidence such as facts and statistics. An **emotional appeal** uses words that bring out strong feelings. An **ethical appeal** uses words that make you think the writer is sincere and qualified to make the remarks.

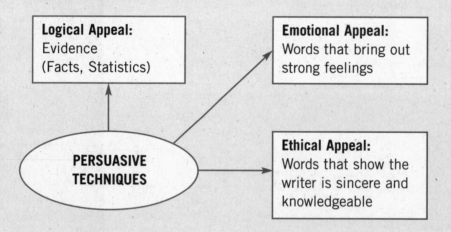

Logical Appeal:
Evidence
(Facts, Statistics)

Emotional Appeal:
Words that bring out
strong feelings

Ethical Appeal:
Words that show the
writer is sincere and
knowledgeable

PERSUASIVE
TECHNIQUES

Into the Essay

Jonathan Swift did not write for fame or money. Most of his books and pamphlets were published without his name as the author. Swift's aim in writing was to change people—to make people kinder and more understanding. *A Modest Proposal* is the most famous of his pamphlets. In it Swift risks appearing to be a monster himself in order to show the monstrous way others behave.

A Modest Proposal

BASED ON THE ESSAY BY
Jonathan Swift

Your
TURN

VOCABULARY

A *burden* (BURD uhn) can be "a heavy load to carry" or "something that you have to put up with." Which meaning does it have in line 2?

_____

_____

_____

_____

_____

_____

_____

_____

_____

_____

Here's
HOW

RECOGNIZING PERSUASIVE TECHNIQUES

In line 12, the narrator says that he has thought about the problem for a long time. This is an ethical appeal. He says he has the knowledge needed to propose a plan that will solve the problem.

YOU NEED TO KNOW This essay, published in 1729, is Jonathan Swift's best and most famous pamphlet. He begins by describing the terrible conditions in Ireland and objecting to the way the English treat the Irish. For three years the Irish harvests had been so poor that farmers got very little money for their crops. The farmers could not pay the rent for their land demanded by their English landlords, who did not live in Ireland. That meant that little money remained to be spent on Irish goods in Ireland. Beggars and starving children were everywhere. Swift argued that England's policies kept the Irish poor. His aim in writing this pamphlet was to change these policies.

In *A Modest Proposal,* Swift offers a solution to these problems—perhaps the most shocking solution ever offered. In this pamphlet he takes on the role of a "practical" economic planner, pretending to use only facts. He seems to be full of common sense, even goodwill. It is this difference between its honest style and its shocking content that gives the pamphlet its force.

A Modest Proposal

FOR PREVENTING THE CHILDREN OF POOR PEOPLE IN IRELAND FROM BEING A BURDEN TO THEIR PARENTS OR COUNTRY, AND FOR MAKING THEM BENEFICIAL TO THE PUBLIC

Walking through the streets of Dublin, or the Irish countryside, it is
5 very sad to see many women begging for food for their families. Each of these women has with her three, four, or even six children, all dressed in rags.

In these difficult times, I think everyone agrees that taking care of all these children is a great burden. For the first year of its life, of
10 course, a baby may be fed cheaply on its mother's milk. But then what?

I have thought very deeply about this problem for a long time, and I have come up with a plan. Under my plan, these children will

not suffer from the need of food and clothing for the rest of their
15 lives. Instead, they will help feed and clothe thousands of others.

I calculate that every year in Ireland a hundred and twenty thousand children are born to parents too poor to take care of them. How can these children be made useful? These days, there is no work for them on farms or in manufacturing. Only the cleverest can make a
20 decent living as a thief before the age of six, although of course most children learn the basics much sooner.

As for selling them as slaves, I have been told by merchants that no one will pay for a boy or girl under twelve years old, and even when they reach this age, they sell for three pounds at most. As the
25 cost of their rags and scraps of food will have added up to at least four times that amount, this earns no profit for their parents or the kingdom.

Therefore, I now humbly suggest my own idea, which I hope will not raise the slightest objection.

30 I have learned that a one-year-old child, well nursed, makes a most delicious, nourishing, and wholesome food. It may be stewed, roasted, baked, or boiled—even fricasseed.

Here is my plan. Of the one hundred twenty thousand poor children born each year, twenty thousand should be kept for breeding,
35 one male for every four females. (This is more than we allow for sheep, cows, or pigs.) The remaining hundred thousand, when they reach one year, shall be sold to wealthy people throughout the kingdom.

Their mothers must let them nurse as much as possible in the last
40 month, to make them plump and fit for a gentleman's table. One twenty-eight-pound child should be enough for two dishes at a dinner party. If the family dines alone, the child will last several meals, and will still be very good on the fourth day, boiled and sprinkled with a little pepper and salt.

45 This food will be somewhat expensive, but very proper for landlords. After all, they have already devoured the parents with the rents they charge; why not the children, too? And, if they are thrifty, they may save the skin to make excellent gloves for ladies and summer boots for fine gentlemen.

VERBAL IRONY

In lines 30–38, the narrator gives a shocking solution to the problem of too many poor children—eating them. He is using irony—saying one thing and meaning another. He actually wants people to take care of the children but says the opposite— that people should eat them, which is cruel and outrageous.

VOCABULARY

I know that *fricasseed* (FRIK uh seed) in line 32 is a cooking method because it is listed with other ways of cooking meat.

RECOGNIZING PERSUASIVE TECHNIQUES

In lines 39–44, the narrator uses two persuasive techniques to convince people that it is all right to eat a child. Look back at the graphic organizer on page 76 to review persuasive techniques. In your text, underline one of the narrator's techniques.

Your TURN

VOCABULARY

Why do you think the narrator uses the word *slaughter* (SLAW tuhr) instead of *kill* in line 56?

_____

_____

_____

_____

Your TURN

VERBAL IRONY

Irony is saying one thing and meaning another. How is the narrator using irony in lines 55–59?

_____

_____

_____

Your TURN

RECOGNIZING PERSUASIVE TECHNIQUES

In lines 69–83, the narrator is using a logical appeal by listing what he says are the advantages that support his plan. Underline three of the advantages.

50   A good friend of mine, and a true lover of his country, recently made another suggestion. He pointed out that many young people between the ages of twelve and fourteen are starving because they cannot find work. Why not use them in place of deer, or venison, for food?

55   But I believe the males would be too tough and lean; and to slaughter the females would be a waste, as they would soon become breeders. Besides, some overly tenderhearted people might consider such a practice almost cruel—and I could never support any project involving the smallest hint of cruelty.

60   What about the vast numbers of poor adults in Ireland who cannot take care of themselves because they are old, sick, or crippled? That problem does not concern me in the least. It is very well known that every day they are dying and rotting, from cold and hunger and filth, as fast as can reasonably be expected.

65   As for the younger people, their condition is almost as hopeful. They cannot find work, and so they cannot eat; then, even if they do get hired accidentally, they are too weak to work. In this way the country's problem will soon be solved.

But back to my subject. I think the advantages of my plan are
70   clear. First, it will greatly cut down on the number of Roman Catholics in Ireland.

Second, the poor tenants will now have valuable property, which landlords can take to pay their rent, since the tenants have no money and their grain and cattle have already been taken away.

75   Third, it will help the economy, as the children will be raised and sold in Ireland, with no need for imports.

Fourth, the breeders will earn money from their children and no longer have to support them after the first year.

Fifth, this popular new dish will draw wealthy customers to
80   taverns where skillful cooks invent the finest recipes.

Sixth, it would encourage mothers to take good care of their children. Men would value their pregnant wives as much as livestock, and would not beat or kick them for fear of causing a miscarriage.

I can think of no objection that could possibly be raised to my
85 plan. Therefore let no one talk to me of other solutions: Taxing the
profits made by absent English landlords, buying clothes and furniture
made only in Ireland, rejecting foreign luxuries and practicing thrift,
learning to love our country and forgetting our political differences,
teaching landlords to show mercy toward their tenants, and
90 shopkeepers becoming honest and hardworking, instead of cheating
everyone.

No, let no one talk to me of such solutions, until there is the least
glimpse of hope that they may be sincerely put into practice.

As for me, I had despaired of ever solving Ireland's problems,
95 until I fortunately came up with my plan. If anyone has another plan
that is equally innocent, cheap, easy, and effective, I would be glad
to hear it. But before anyone rejects my idea, let them answer two
questions.

First, as things now stand, how will Ireland find food and clothing
100 for a hundred thousand useless mouths and backs? And second, I
would like the absentee landlords to ask the poor of Ireland whether
they would not have been happier to be sold for food at a year old,
than to have suffered the endless hunger, the lack of clothing and
shelter, the impossibility of paying rent without money or work, and
105 the certainty of passing this miserable life down to their children.

My only motive in making this proposal is to help my country
by improving our trade, providing for babies, helping the poor, and
giving some pleasure to the rich. I cannot hope to earn a single
penny, as my youngest child is nine years old, and my wife is too old
110 to have more.

VOCABULARY

What is the meaning of the word *solutions* (suh LOO shuhns) in lines 85 and 92? Can you think of another meaning of this word?

_____

_____

_____

RECOGNIZING PERSUASIVE TECHNIQUES

In lines 99-105, the narrator uses words and phrases that bring out the emotions of the reader. Some of these are "useless mouths and backs," "sold for food," "suffered the endless hunger," "lack of clothing and shelter," and "miserable life."

VERBAL IRONY

Why is the narrator's statement in lines 106–108 ironic?

_____

_____

_____

_____

Irony

Irony is the contrast or difference between what you expect to hear or see and what actually happens. There are several kinds of irony. The two kinds listed below are particularly relevant to this essay:

- In **verbal irony** what is said contrasts with what is actually meant to be understood.
- **Situational irony** is a contrast between what is expected to happen and what actually does happen.

1. The paragraph beginning "I have learned that a one-year-old child, . . . " (line 30) introduces the main **situational irony** of the essay. Explain what you expected the narrator to suggest at first and what he *really* suggested.

   I expected a sensible proposal to solve the problem. Instead, the narrator proposes

   slaughter and cannibalism.

2. Why is the word *hopeful* (line 65) an example of verbal irony? What does *hopeful* really mean in this sentence?

   _____

   _____

   _____

3. In the final paragraph the speaker claims that he is offering his proposal for the good of Ireland. What is ironic about this claim? What does the speaker really mean?

   _____

   _____

   _____

Vocabulary Development

Word Analogies

An **analogy** is a likeness between two things that are unlike in other ways. When you state an analogy, you compare two things to show how they are alike. A **word analogy** is a written statement that compares two pairs of words.

Reading word analogies. In a word analogy the relationship between the first pair of words is the same as the relationship between the second pair of words. For example, *cool* and *chilly* have the same relationship to each other that *mad* and *angry* have. Here's how a word analogy is usually written:

COOL: CHILLY :: mad : angry

The colon (:) stands for the phrase "is related to." The double colon (::) between the two pairs of words stands for the phrase "in the same way that." Here are two ways to read the analogy:

COOL [is related to] CHILLY [in the same way that] *mad* [is related to] *angry*.

COOL is to CHILLY as *mad* is to *angry*.

Solving word analogies. Use the following steps to solve an analogy question:

- Identify the relationship between the capitalized pair of words. For example, are the words synonyms (alike) or antonyms (opposites)?
- Look for the same relationship in the pairs of words in the answer choices. Eliminate those that do not have that relationship.
- Choose the pair of words whose relationship and word order match those of the capitalized pair.

For each of the following items, choose the pair of words that expresses a relationship that is most similar to the relationship between the pair of capitalized words:

1. BURDEN : LOAD ::
   a. dark : light
   b. disease : illness
   c. education : college
   d. advantage : disadvantage

2. SOLUTIONS : PROBLEMS ::
   a. destiny : fate
   b. opportunities : chances
   c. followers : supporters
   d. safety : danger

from Don Quixote

Literary Focus: Parody

A literary **parody** is an imitation of a work of literature for amusement or instruction. Parodies often make the characteristics of someone or something seem silly or ridiculous. To do this, parodies use exaggeration, humorous imitation, and verbal irony (saying one thing and meaning another). Parodies also match up things that don't go together. For example, in the excerpt you're about to read, you will see that Don Quixote and his servant, Sancho Panza, make a mismatched pair because they are nothing alike.

Reading Skill: Making Inferences

Inferences are educated guesses based on information in the text and what you already know. When you read a story, you fill in missing information, reading between the lines to make guesses about what's left unsaid.

Into the Story

In *Don Quixote,* Cervantes makes fun of medieval tales of chivalry and courtly love. These stories often involved knights who fought monsters and went on quests, or journeys, to please the women they adored. These stories were still very popular during the 1500s, when Cervantes lived.

FROM
Don Quixote
Miguel de Cervantes

BASED ON THE NOVEL TRANSLATED BY
John Ormsby

Here's HOW

PARODY

I think Don Quixote's attack on the windmills is an example of humorous imitation, one of the characteristics of parody. Traditionally, knights battled other knights, so this episode is making fun of that aspect of chivalry.

YOU NEED TO KNOW Don Quixote is a middle-aged man who has become lost in a fantasy world because he spends all of his time reading medieval books about knights and chivalry. He decides to become a knight himself and search for adventure. He takes down his family's rusty armor and names his bony old horse Rocinante. He knows that as a knight he must have a lady to whom he can dedicate his dangerous adventures. He chooses a country girl whom he hardly knows and calls her Dulcinea. Don Quixote meets a poor farmer named Sancho Panza in his home town whom he convinces to become his helper.

The excerpt you are about to read tells what happens when Don Quixote and Sancho Panza see thirty or forty windmills on one of their adventures.

from Don Quixote
based on the John Ormsby
translation of Miguel de Cervantes's masterpiece

from Chapter 8

About Don Quixote's good luck in the scary windmill adventure and related events.

Suddenly, Don Quixote and his assistant Sancho Panza noticed
5 thirty or forty windmills on the plain in front of them. Instead of windmills, though, Don Quixote thought he saw evil giants, so he decided to go into battle against them. Sancho Panza tried to stop him. He explained to his master that they were facing windmills with long blades that turned in the wind, but Don Quixote insisted they
10 were facing monsters with long arms.

"Clearly, you don't know much about this kind of adventure," he said to his assistant. "If you're afraid, stay behind and pray. I'll do the fighting."

Then he spurred his horse Rocinante and charged toward the
15 windmills. Even when he got close, he still thought the windmills were living giants and shouted insults at them. Next, the windmill

blades began to turn in the wind, but Don Quixote thought the "giants" were threatening him with many arms. Then, thinking of his lady Dulcinea to give him courage, Don Quixote rushed into battle
20 against the windmills. He charged at the first one so fast that its whirling blades broke his lance and threw him and his horse to the ground.

Quickly, Sancho Panza came to his master's rescue, insisting again that Don Quixote had attacked windmills instead of monsters. This
25 time, Quixote agreed with his assistant, but he was sure that his enemy, a magician named Friston, had turned the giants into windmills as he charged at them.

Sancho Panza helped his master back onto his horse, and the two rode off down the Puerto Lapice highway in search of further
30 adventures. Missing his broken lance, Don Quixote remembered the story of a knight named Diego Perez de Vargas.

"When this knight broke his sword in battle," Quixote told his assistant, "he made a club from a heavy oak branch and pounded his enemies with it in battle. He was so successful with his club that
35 everyone started calling him Machuca, the Pounder." Then Quixote announced that he, too, would find a club and use it so successfully against his enemies that Sancho Panza would feel lucky to be his companion in these adventures. Sancho Panza humored his master by acting as if he believed what Quixote told him.

40 As they rode along, Sancho Panza noticed that Quixote was slipping in his saddle and worried that his recent fall had left him shaken. Quixote agreed but said that a true knight would not complain about his injuries, no matter what. Being more realistic, Sancho Panza said that he himself would complain over the smallest
45 injury. His master laughed and said that the rules of chivalry would allow a knight's assistant to complain as often as he wanted to.

It was time for the two men to eat. Don Quixote was not hungry, but he didn't mind Sancho Panza eating, so his assistant made himself comfortable on the donkey he was riding and began to eat
50 and to take huge swigs from his flask. Sancho Panza kept his good sense of humor as he rode along, eating and drinking. He was willing to go along with his master, regardless of the hazards.

MAKING INFERENCES

In lines 23–27, Sancho Panza finally convinces Don Quixote that he was battling windmills, not monsters. What can you infer about Sancho Panza's character from his actions?

_____

_____

_____

VOCABULARY

The word *club* (line 33) can mean "an organization," "a suit of playing cards," or "a heavy stick used as a weapon." Which meaning does *club* have in this passage? What context clues help you to determine its meaning?

_____

_____

_____

PARODY

Don Quixote makes a point of following the rules of chivalry. In lines 40–59, what two specific rules does he follow? What sacrifices does he make in order to follow these rules?

_____

_____

_____

That night as they camped along the road, Don Quixote replaced his broken lance with a branch from one of the trees around them. He
55 had read that adventuring knights always stayed awake at night remembering their sweethearts, so Don Quixote went without sleep, thinking of Dulcinea instead. Sancho Panza slept. He had a full stomach and had had nothing to keep him awake. He slept so deeply that when morning came, neither sunlight nor bird song awoke him.
60 When Don Quixote called out to him, Sancho Panza awoke and took a deep drink from his flask. It worried him to see how little was left in the flask because he didn't think there would be a chance to refill it soon. Don Quixote didn't have breakfast; his memories of Dulcinea were enough for him. Then the two adventurers set out
65 upon the road again.

That afternoon, they arrived at Puerto Lapice. When Don Quixote saw the city on the road before them, he got excited about the adventures they would have there. He warned Sancho Panza not to defend him if he got into a fight with high-ranking men. The rules of
70 chivalry said that only another knight could assist him in a fight with someone of his rank. He told Sancho Panza, though, that the assistant could come to his aid in a fight with men of lower rank.

Sancho Panza replied that he would obey his master's request, explaining that he was a peaceful sort anyway and didn't like to
75 interfere in the quarrels of others. He added that if attacked himself, he would of course fight. "The universal rules of self-defense allow it," he said.

Don Quixote agreed but reminded Sancho Panza not to interfere if his master got into a fight with men of his own rank. Finally, Sancho
80 Panza promised to go along with this request.

Parody

A **parody** is an imitation of a work of literature for amusement or instruction. Parodies often make the characteristics of someone or something seem ridiculous. To do this, parodies typically use four types of devices:

- exaggeration
- verbal irony (saying one thing and meaning another)
- incongruity (pairing things that don't belong together)
- humorous imitation

Fill in the chart below with at least one example of each of these devices from *Don Quixote:*

Devices Used in Parody	Examples
1. exaggeration	
2. verbal irony	
3. incongruity	
4. humorous imitation	

The Romantic Period
1798–1832

In the spring of 1798, two young British poets sold some of their poems. Samuel Taylor Coleridge, aged 25, and William Wordsworth, 27, needed to raise money for a trip to Germany. Soon after they left Britain, their book, *Lyrical Ballads and a Few Other Poems*, was
5 published. Among the "few other poems" was Coleridge's *The Rime of the Ancient Mariner* and Wordsworth's "Lines Composed a Few Miles Above Tintern Abbey." These works are now among the most important poems in British literature. At the time, though, no one knew that *Lyrical Ballads* would usher in a new literary age.

10 This age, known as the Romantic period, would produce six major poets: William Blake; William Wordsworth; Samuel Taylor Coleridge; George Gordon, Lord Byron; Percy Bysshe Shelley; and John Keats.

Turbulent Times, Bitter Realities

The Romantic period was a turbulent one, both in Britain and abroad.
15 Britain was changing rapidly from a farming society into an industrial one. A new working class was growing restless in overcrowded mill towns. The American colonies had recently rebelled against British rule and won their independence.

Across the English Channel, truly terrifying events had been
20 taking place. In 1789, the French people had overthrown their king, Louis XVI. What began as a hopeful movement toward democracy quickly turned bloody. Hundreds of French aristocrats were beheaded. The government, now in chaos, was seized by a man named Napoleon Bonaparte—first as dictator and then as emperor.

25 All of these events made British conservatives nervous. These supporters of the king feared that a revolution would occur in Britain, too. To prevent such a thing, the government passed harsh new laws. It also fought a war against Napoleon, finally defeating him in a battle at Waterloo, Belgium, in 1815.

30 British conservatives believed this victory saved their country from a tyrant. But British liberals did not. Like Wordsworth, they supported

the democratic ideals of the French Revolution. They saw Waterloo as
the defeat of one tyrant by another.

The Tyranny of Laissez Faire

35   The Industrial Revolution was bringing about other changes in British
life. Goods once made by hand were now being produced in factories.
Land once shared by farmers was now being taken over by single
owners. Many people who lost their land went to the cities to look for
work. The cities grew rapidly, and living conditions worsened.

40   In short, the rich grew richer and the poor grew poorer. The
economic idea that allowed this to happen was called *laissez faire.*
(LEHS ay FAIR) These French words mean "let people do as they
please." In economic terms this meant that buying and selling should
be allowed to happen without government interference. Such a system

45   was very hard on the helpless and the young. Poor children were
often forced to work in factories or coal mines, harnessed to coal carts
like animals.

        Under *laissez faire* the government was unwilling to step in and
help. Unhappy with the "powers that be," the Romantic poets staged

50   a poetic revolution. They rejected the public, formal poetry of the
1700s. Instead, they wrote lyric poetry that was private, free flowing,
and emotional. These poets used the imagination rather than reason
to respond to the rapid changes of the time.

What Does "Romantic" Mean?

55   Today the word *romantic* often describes feelings of love. In literature,
however, the word *romantic* comes from the term *romance.* The
romance was a popular form of literature in the Middle Ages. It
featured adventure, mystery, and fearless heroes. The Romantic
writers sometimes used elements of the romance in their own works.

60   It is for *this* reason—not because they wrote love poems—that they
are known as the "Romantic" poets.

        The term *romantic* also has other meanings that relate to the
Romantic poets. First, it can involve an interest in youth and
innocence. Second, it can refer to a time when people begin to

VOCABULARY

The word *tyrant* in line 33
means "a cruel ruler." Re-read
lines 25–29. What two people
is the writer referring to as
tyrants?

_____

_____

_____

VOCABULARY

Underline the definitions of
laissez faire in lines 40–47.
Then, name at least two groups
of people the *laissez faire*
policy affected.

_____

_____

_____

_____

_____

65 question old ways and to imagine newer, better ways to live. Third, it can refer to a time of great change during which people are forced to adapt. During the first half of the 1800s, the rise of industry created just such a change. The Romantic poets called upon people to accept these changes rather than resist them.

Poetry, Nature, and the Imagination

70 In 1800, Wordsworth wrote a preface for a new edition of *Lyrical Ballads*. In it he declared that he was writing a new kind of poetry— poetry that was the "spontaneous overflow of powerful feelings." These **lyric poems** used ordinary language to describe common

75 subjects—such as country life. In the country, Wordsworth wrote, "the passions of men are incorporated with . . . Nature."

The Romantics were intrigued by the ways in which nature and the human mind, or imagination, acted upon one another. Each of the Romantic poets saw this relationship differently. However, for all of

80 them, nature moved the imagination in powerful ways. Once moved, they thought, the imagination became a powerful force of its own. Like the power of God, it worked to create new realities—new poems, new societies, and perhaps a new, more perfect world.

The Idea of the Poet

85 In 1802, yet another edition of *Lyrical Ballads* was published. This time, Wordsworth added a long section to the 1800 Preface. The new section tried to answer the question *What is a poet?* Wordsworth's answer began: "He is a man speaking to men."

This kind of speaking was not the reasoned, witty language of

90 the eighteenth-century verse. Instead, it was the natural, emotional language of the heart—the language you might hear in a private conversation. Such language is still being used in poetry today.

Wordsworth's idea of the poet as "a man speaking to men" was new in several ways. For one, it was a democratic idea. The speaker

95 is a common person—not a person above or apart from the rest. In these poems the speaker has an experience that all people have. He or

she sees something in nature (or another person), responds, and is deeply changed by it.

The Romantic Poet

100　In saying that the poet is "a man speaking to men," Wordsworth did not mean that the poet is just anyone. The poet is a special person, one who possesses "a greater knowledge of human nature" than most. Indeed, all of the Romantic poets thought highly of the poet's role. William Blake saw the poet as an inspired teacher. Coleridge

105　wrote that the poet "brings the whole soul of man into activity." Shelley called poets "the unacknowledged legislators of the world." Keats saw the poet as a "physician" to humanity.

　　　The poet, in sum, is someone we cannot do without.

What Was Romanticism?

- The Romantics turned away from reason and formality and embraced imagination and naturalness.
- The Romantic poets rejected the public, formal, and witty works of the 1700s. Their lyric poems were personal and emotional, and their language was simple.
- Wordsworth proposed a new, democratic idea of poetry. Although the poet had special abilities, he was also "a man speaking to men."
- Many Romantics turned to the past or to the imagination, away from industrial society.
- Most Romantics believed in democracy and opposed tyranny.
- For the Romantics, nature and the human mind mirrored each other. Nature also had the power to change the human mind profoundly.

VOCABULARY

The word *role* in line 104 can mean "a part played by an actor in a play," or "purpose or proper work." What do you think is the correct meaning of *role* in this sentence? Explain your answer.

_____

_____

_____

_____

VOCABULARY

What do you think is the meaning of the phrase *in sum* in line 108? Explain your answer.

_____

_____

_____

_____

Lines Composed a Few Miles Above Tintern Abbey

Literary Focus: Blank Verse

This famous poem is written in **blank verse,** or unrhymed **iambic** (y AM bihk) **pentameter** (pehn TAM uh tuhr). **Blank** means that the poetry does not rhyme. An **iamb** is one unstressed syllable followed by one stressed syllable (da DAH). **Pentameter** means that each line of verse has five feet, that is, five iambs (da DAH, da DAH, da DAH, da DAH, da DAH). This style of poetry comes close to sounding like ordinary speech.

Reading Skill: Recognizing Patterns of Organization

Before you read the poem, look for the end punctuation and indentions that tell you that one stanza, or **verse paragraph,** is ending and another is beginning. There are five stanzas in the poem. Wordsworth used the stanzas to organize his ideas. Another way to recognize Wordsworth's organization is to break down long sentences into smaller parts.

Into the Poem

William Wordsworth was tired of the kind of poetry that was witty, satirical, and intellectual. He wanted to break free of this style of poetry and write about his personal feelings. Wordsworth loved nature in all of its forms, and he believed that nature helped him to "see into the life of things." He wrote this poem after a four-day walking tour, part of which was through the valley of the Wye River in southern Wales. It is one of the most important short poems expressing feeling in English literature.

Lines Composed a Few Miles Above Tintern Abbey

William Wordsworth

Here's
HOW

BLANK VERSE

I see that there are ten syllables each in lines 1 and 2 of the poem. However, the lines do not rhyme—*length* and *hear* are not rhyming words. Blank verse does not rhyme.

Your
TURN

RECOGNIZING PATTERNS OF ORGANIZATION

Stanzas in blank verse are not all the same length. What visual clue tells you that one stanza is ending and another one is beginning?

_____

_____

_____

YOU NEED TO KNOW   This lyric poem is a meditation on what the Wye River valley in Wales has meant to the speaker. This valley stands for all of nature in the poem. He first describes the physical beauty of the valley, seen after a five-year absence. He then explains how his youthful, emotional response has changed, becoming deeper and more thoughtful. He is glad that he no longer has to be physically in a natural setting to receive nature's healing powers. His memories can lift his spirits and inspire him to acts of kindness at any time or in any place. Finally, the speaker addresses his sister, saying that having her with him makes the landscape even more precious to him.

Five years have past; five summers, with the length
Of five long winters! and again I hear
These waters, rolling from their mountain springs
With a soft inland murmur.—Once again
5 Do I behold these steep and lofty cliffs,
That on a wild secluded scene impress
Thoughts of more deep seclusion; and connect
The landscape with the quiet of the sky.
The day is come when I again repose
10 Here, under this dark sycamore, and view
These plots of cottage ground, these orchard tufts,
Which at this season, with their unripe fruits,
Are clad in one green hue, and lose themselves
'Mid groves and copses.[1] Once again I see
15 These hedgerows,[2] hardly hedgerows, little lines
Of sportive wood run wild: these pastoral farms,
Green to the very door; and wreaths of smoke
Sent up, in silence, from among the trees!
With some uncertain notice, as might seem
20 Of vagrant dwellers in the houseless woods,
Or of some Hermit's cave, where by his fire
The Hermit sits alone.

---

1. **copses:** areas densely covered with shrubs and small trees.
2. **hedgerows:** rows of bushes, shrubs, and small trees that serve as fences.

IN OTHER WORDS It's been five years since I've been here. I again hear the sound of the river flowing down from the mountains. Once again I see these steep, high cliffs, which make me think of being completely alone. These cliffs connect the landscape to the quiet sky. I rest here, under a dark sycamore tree, and look out at the farmland and the orchards. It is not the season for ripe fruit—all the fruit trees are the same green color, blending into the woods. Once again I see the hedgerows, which are hardly even proper hedgerows—just lines of woods running wild. I see the farmhouses, with plants growing right up to their doors. I see smoke rising silently from among the trees. I imagine the smoke to come from the fire of a homeless person living in the woods or from the cave of a hermit who sits alone.

> These beauteous forms,
> Through a long absence, have not been to me
> As is a landscape to a blind man's eye:
> 25 But oft, in lonely rooms, and 'mid the din
> Of towns and cities, I have owed to them
> In hours of weariness, sensations sweet,
> Felt in the blood, and felt along the heart;
> And passing even into my purer mind,
> 30 With tranquil restoration:—feelings too
> Of unremembered pleasure: such, perhaps,
> As have no slight or trivial influence
> On that best portion of a good man's life,
> His little, nameless, unremembered acts
> 35 Of kindness and of love. Nor less, I trust,
> To them I may have owed another gift,
> Of aspect more sublime; that blessed mood,
> In which the burden of the mystery,
> In which the heavy and the weary weight
> 40 Of all this unintelligible world,

BLANK VERSE

I see that line 29 has eleven syllables, instead of ten. Blank verse is supposed to have ten syllables. The rhythm will be correct in this line if I pronounce the word *even* as if it had only one syllable—*e'en*.

Is lightened:—that serene and blessed mood,

In which the affections³ gently lead us on,—

Until, the breath of this corporeal⁴ frame

And even the motion of our human blood

45 Almost suspended, we are laid asleep

In body, and become a living soul:

While with an eye made quiet by the power

Of harmony, and the deep power of joy,

We see into the life of things.

IN OTHER WORDS   Even though I've been gone a long time, I could still see these beautiful sights in my mind's eye. When I've been tired, sitting alone in my room or surrounded by the noise of a city, the memory of this place has given me good feelings. These emotions run through my blood and my heart, into my mind, giving me peace and new energy. Perhaps these feelings will strongly influence me to perform small acts of kindness and love. These memories have restored my balance and made me a kinder, more generous person. They have led me to a blessed mood in which I begin to see more clearly the meaning of life. In that peaceful mood we hardly breathe, our blood hardly moves, and our whole body seems almost asleep. We feel as if we were souls without bodies. The harmony and joy we have received from Nature lets us see into the quiet life of things.

                                            If this

50 Be but a vain belief, yet, oh! how oft—

In darkness and amid the many shapes

Of joyless daylight; when the fretful stir

Unprofitable, and the fever of the world,

Have hung upon the beatings of my heart—

---

3. **affections:** feelings.
4. **corporeal** (kawr PAWR ee uhl): bodily.

55 How oft, in spirit, have I turned to thee,
O sylvan[5] Wye! thou wanderer through the woods,
How often has my spirit turned to thee!

IN OTHER WORDS Perhaps what I believe is not true.
And yet, in the nights and days when the rushing, busy world
has made me sick and unhappy, how many times have I
returned to you. You, the River Wye, who wander through the
woods—how often, in my mind, have I turned to you!

    And now, with gleams of half-extinguished thought,
With many recognitions dim and faint,
60 And somewhat of a sad perplexity,
The picture of the mind[6] revives again:
While here I stand, not only with the sense
Of present pleasure, but with pleasing thoughts
That in this moment there is life and food
65 For future years. And so I dare to hope,
Though changed, no doubt, from what I was when first
I came among these hills; when like a roe[7]
I bounded o'er the mountains, by the sides
Of the deep rivers, and the lonely streams,
70 Wherever nature led: more like a man
Flying from something that he dreads, than one
Who sought the thing he loved. For nature then
(The coarser pleasures of my boyish days,
And their glad animal movements all gone by)
75 To me was all in all.—I cannot paint
What then I was. The sounding cataract[8]
Haunted me like a passion: the tall rock,
The mountain, and the deep and gloomy wood,

Here's HOW

RECOGNIZING PATTERNS OF ORGANIZATION

Lines 66-84 are like a flashback in a story. The speaker is telling how he felt about the landscape in the past. He loved nature and did lots of hiking. But it was as if he were running away from something he hated, rather than going toward something he loved. A big clue to this is in line 83, when the speaker says, "That time is past."

---

5. **sylvan** (SIHL vuhn): associated with the forest or woodlands.
6. **picture of the mind:** primarily the picture in the mind, but also the picture the individual mind has of itself.
7. **roe:** deer.
8. **cataract** (KAT uh rakt): waterfall.

Your TURN

BLANK VERSE

Line 92 has eleven syllables, instead of the ten that are usual for blank verse. How can you pronounce the word *power* differently to keep the rhythm and pace of blank verse? (Hint: Look back at how *even* can be pronounced in line 29.)

_____

_____

_____

_____

Your TURN

RECOGNIZING PATTERNS OF ORGANIZATION

In lines 102–110, the speaker is summarizing the main idea of this stanza. In your own words, give the main idea.

_____

_____

_____

_____

_____

_____

_____

Their colors and their forms, were then to me

80 An appetite; a feeling and a love,

That had no need of a remoter charm,[9]

By thought supplied, nor any interest

Unborrowed from the eye— That time is past,

And all its aching joys are now no more.

85 And all its dizzy raptures. Not for this

Faint[10] I, nor mourn nor murmur; other gifts

Have followed; for such loss, I would believe,

Abundant recompense.[11] For I have learned

To look on nature, not as in the hour

90 Of thoughtless youth; but hearing oftentimes

The still, sad music of humanity,

Nor harsh nor grating, though of ample power

To chasten and subdue. And I have felt

A presence that disturbs me with the joy

95 Of elevated thoughts; a sense sublime

Of something far more deeply interfused,

Whose dwelling is the light of setting suns,

And the round ocean and the living air,

And the blue sky, and in the mind of man:

100 A motion and a spirit, that impels

All thinking things, all objects of all thought,

And rolls through all things. Therefore am I still

A lover of the meadows and the woods,

And mountains; and of all that we behold

105 From this green earth; of all the mighty world

Of eye, and ear—both what they half create,

And what perceive; well pleased to recognize

In nature and the language of the sense

The anchor of my purest thoughts, the nurse,

110 The guide, the guardian of my heart, and soul

Of all my moral being.

---

9. **remoter charm:** appeal other than the scene itself.
10. **faint:** become weak; lose heart.
11. **recompense** (REHK uhm pehns): repayment.

IN OTHER WORDS   Now, this scene which I have pictured so often is here before me again in reality, although not exactly the way I remembered it. I stand here, enjoying not just the scene but also the thought of how the memory of this moment will give me pleasure in years to come. That is my hope. When I was young, I loved the natural world with a passion. I did lots of hiking. I accepted what I saw at face value. I did not look below the surface. I was more like a man running away from something I dreaded than like one seeking the things I love. I was no longer a boy, with the joy of a wild animal. Nature was everything to me then—I can't describe what I was like. The noise of a waterfall haunted me like a passion. The tall rock, the mountain, the deep wood, their colors and shapes, were something I hungered for. The feeling was immediate and direct. It didn't need any deep thought, anything other than what I saw in front of me.

That time is gone. Its painful joys and dizzy thrills are no more. I don't mourn it; time has brought me other gifts, which make up for that loss. I've learned to look at nature in a different way than I did as a thoughtless young man. Now, I hear the quiet, sad music of humanity. It isn't harsh, though it has the power to make me quiet and humble. And I have felt a presence that fills me with the joy of higher thoughts. I have felt a sense of something holy, which lives in the light of setting suns, in the ocean and the air, in the blue sky, and in the mind of man. It is a motion and a spirit, which draws to itself all thinking things and all things that are thought about and is in everything.

So I still love the meadows, woods, and mountains, everything there is to see and hear on earth. I love both what is there and what I add to it with my thoughts and understanding. I am pleased to see that nature and my own senses are what make me my best self. They are like an anchor, a nurse, a guide, a guardian for my soul.

I can see that, in lines 111-115, the speaker changes from talking to himself to talking to his sister, Dorothy. This final stanza now has a different main idea.

Your
TURN

BLANK VERSE

Read lines 116–134 aloud as you walk. Then, select two lines that you like the best, and write down the words you are saying when you step with your leading foot.

_____

_____

_____

_____

_____

_____

_____

_____

_____

_____

_____

_____

_____

_____

_____

Nor perchance,
If I were not thus taught, should I the more
Suffer[12] my genial[13] spirits to decay:
For thou art with me here upon the banks

115 Of this fair river; thou my dearest Friend,[14]
My dear, dear Friend; and in thy voice I catch
The language of my former heart, and read
My former pleasures in the shooting lights
Of thy wild eyes. Oh! yet a little while

120 May I behold in thee what I was once,
My dear, dear Sister! and this prayer I make,
Knowing that Nature never did betray
The heart that loved her; 'tis her privilege,
Through all the years of this our life, to lead

125 From joy to joy: for she can so inform
The mind that is within us, so impress
With quietness and beauty, and so feed
With lofty thoughts, that neither evil tongues,
Rash judgments, nor the sneers of selfish men,

130 Nor greetings where no kindness is, nor all
The dreary intercourse[15] of daily life,
Shall e'er prevail against us, or disturb
Our cheerful faith, that all which we behold
Is full of blessings. Therefore let the moon

135 Shine on thee in thy solitary walk;
And let the misty mountain winds be free
To blow against thee: and, in after years,
When these wild ecstasies shall be matured
Into a sober pleasure; when thy mind

140 Shall be a mansion for all lovely forms,
Thy memory be as a dwelling place
For all sweet sounds and harmonies; oh! then,
If solitude, or fear, or pain, or grief,

---

12. **suffer:** allow.
13. **genial** (JEEN yuhl): creative.
14. **my dearest Friend:** Wordsworth's sister, Dorothy.
15. **intercourse:** dealings; social contacts.

Should be thy portion, with what healing thoughts
145 Of tender joy wilt thou remember me,
And these my exhortations![16] Nor, perchance—
If I should be where I no more can hear
Thy voice, nor catch from thy wild eyes these gleams
Of past existence—wilt thou then forget
150 That on the banks of this delightful stream
We stood together; and that I, so long
A worshipper of Nature, hither came
Unwearied in that service: rather say
With warmer love—oh! with far deeper zeal
155 Of holier love. Nor wilt thou then forget
That after many wanderings, many years
Of absence, these steep woods and lofty cliffs,
And this green pastoral[17] landscape, were to me
More dear, both for themselves and for thy sake!

Here's HOW

BLANK VERSE

When I get to the end of the poem, I see that the poet does not rhyme the last two lines. I think that would be a good way to close the poem. Maybe he doesn't need to make these lines rhyme because the thoughts themselves give a feeling of finality, or completion.

IN OTHER WORDS Even without this teaching, I would not allow my creative spirit to go away. For you are here with me on the banks of this beautiful river, my dearest friend. In your voice I hear the language my heart once spoke. In the light of your eyes I see the pleasure I used to feel. Oh, for just a little while, may I see in you, my dear sister, what I used to be. Nature does not betray those who love her. It is her privilege to lead us from joy to joy, through all the years of our lives. Nature has the ability to affect our minds with quiet beauty and high thoughts, so that neither human unkindness nor the depressing events of daily life can bring us down or shake our faith that life is full of blessings.

---

16. exhortations (EHG zawr TAY shuhnz): strong advice.
17. pastoral (PAS tuhr uhl): relating to herds or flocks, pasture land, and country life.

Let the moon shine on you as you walk alone, and let the misty mountain winds blow against you. In later years, when beautiful sights and sounds live only in your memory—then, if you should be lonely, or afraid, or suffering, remember me and my words with healing thoughts of joy. If I have gone where I can no longer hear your voice or see in your eyes glimmers from my past, do not forget that we stood together on the banks of this delightful river. Remember that I, who have worshiped Nature for so long, did not tire of my service. In fact, my love for Nature was even warmer, deeper, and holier. Do not forget, either, that after many years away from these deep woods and high cliffs and this green country landscape, they were even more dear to me—both for their own sake and for yours!

Blank Verse

Blank verse is poetry written in unrhymed **iambic pentameter.** Most lines contain five iambs; each iamb, or metrical foot, consists of an unstressed syllable (˘) followed by a stressed syllable (′).

Example: The day is come when I again repose

Wordsworth does not always follow this pattern of stressed and unstressed syllables. Lines 4 and 5 are an example where Wordsworth varies this pattern.

With a soft inland murmur.—Once again

Do I behold these steep and lofty cliffs,

Wordsworth organizes his blank verse into groups of lines called **verse paragraphs.** These lines develop a **main idea.** In the first verse paragraph (lines 1–22), the main idea is expressed in the description of the scene—a place in nature to which the speaker has returned after five years.

Re-read aloud one of the verse paragraphs whose lines are given below, watching out for the punctuation and **run-on lines:**

Verse Paragraph 2: Lines 22–49
Verse Paragraph 3: Lines 49–57
Verse Paragraph 4: Lines 58–111
Verse Paragraph 5: Lines 111–159

Then, on the lines below, write a few sentences stating whether you think the verse paragraph you have chosen is unified by **one main idea.** If so, state the main idea.

_____

_____

_____

_____

_____

_____

_____

_____

Kubla Khan

Literary Focus: Alliteration

Alliteration is the repetition of consonant sounds in words that are close together. In this poem, alliteration helps create a dreamy, enchanted mood. The title, "Kubla Khan," itself is an example of alliteration. An example from the poem is the line "Five <u>m</u>iles <u>m</u>eandering with a <u>m</u>azy <u>m</u>otion."

Alliteration is based on the *sound,* not on the *spelling* of the word. Notice that all of the following words have the *k* sound: <u>q</u>uaint, <u>c</u>urtain, <u>k</u>ing.

Reading Skill: Responding to the Text

Take notes as you read the poem or as someone reads it aloud. You may want to describe the images you see or note the questions you would like to ask the poet. Does this poem put you in a certain mood or state of mind? Remember that there is no "right" response to a poem—everyone has his or her own idea of what a poem is about.

Into the Poem

Samuel Taylor Coleridge is trying to capture dreams or visions in this poem. You should focus on feeling the mood of the poem rather than trying to figure out what each image or symbol means. Coleridge thought that literature was a magical mixture of thought and emotion.

Kubla Khan

Samuel Taylor Coleridge

Kubla Khan

In Xanadu did Kubla Khan
A stately pleasure-dome decree:
Where Alph,[1] the sacred river, ran
Through caverns measureless to man
5   Down to a sunless sea.
So twice five miles of fertile ground
With walls and towers were girdled round:
And there were gardens bright with sinuous rills,[2]
Where blossomed many an incense-bearing tree;
10 And here were forests ancient as the hills,
Enfolding sunny spots of greenery.

But oh! that deep romantic chasm which slanted
Down the green hill athwart a cedarn cover![3]
A savage place! as holy and enchanted
15 As e'er beneath a waning moon was haunted
By woman wailing for her demon-lover!
And from this chasm, with ceaseless turmoil seething,
As if this earth in fast thick pants were breathing,
A mighty fountain momently[4] was forced:
20 Amid whose swift half-intermitted burst
Huge fragments vaulted like rebounding hail,
Or chaffy grain beneath the thresher's flail:[5]
And 'mid these dancing rocks at once and ever
It flung up momently the sacred river.
25 Five miles meandering with a mazy[6] motion
Through wood and dale the sacred river ran,
Then reached the caverns measureless to man,
And sank in tumult to a lifeless ocean:
And 'mid this tumult Kubla heard from far
30 Ancestral voices prophesying war!
     The shadow of the dome of pleasure

---

1. **Alph:** probably a reference to the Greek river Alpheus, which flows into the Ionian Sea, and whose waters are fabled to rise up again in Sicily.
2. **sinuous** (SIHN yu uhs) **rills:** winding streams.
3. **athwart a cedarn cover:** crossing diagonally under a covering growth of cedar trees.
4. **momently:** at each moment.
5. **thresher's flail:** heavy, whiplike tool used to thresh, or beat, grain in order to separate the kernels from their chaff, or husks.
6. **mazy:** like a maze; having many turns.

Floated midway on the waves;

Where was heard the mingled measure[7]

From the fountain and the caves.

35 It was a miracle of rare device,

A sunny pleasure-dome with caves of ice!

A damsel with a dulcimer[8]

In a vision once I saw:

It was an Abyssinian[9] maid,

40 And on her dulcimer she played,

Singing of Mount Abora.[10]

Could I revive within me

Her symphony and song,

To such a deep delight 'twould win me,

45 That with music loud and long,

I would build that dome in air,

That sunny dome! those caves of ice!

And all who heard should see them there,

And all should cry, Beware! Beware!

50 His flashing eyes, his floating hair!

Weave a circle round him thrice,

And close your eyes with holy dread,

For he on honeydew hath fed,

And drunk the milk of Paradise.

IN OTHER WORDS   The speaker states that Kubla Khan built a pleasure dome, or palace, in Xanadu. It is surrounded by gardens, forests, and streams. Deep in a valley a fountain bursts forth, sending the sacred river Alph into a lifeless sea. Khan hears voices in the fountain, foretelling war. The speaker sees a vision of a young maiden. He says that, if he could recapture her music, he would be able to rebuild the pleasure dome at Xanadu. People would then hold him in fear and awe, as if he were a god.

---

7. **measure:** rhythmic sound.
8. **dulcimer** (DUHL suh muhr): musical instrument that is often played by striking the strings with small hammers.
9. **Abyssinian** (AB uh SIHN ee uhn): Ethiopian. Ethiopia is in northeast Africa.
10. **Mount Abora:** probably a reference to John Milton's (1608–1674) *Paradise Lost*, in which Mount Amara, in Ethiopia, is a mythical, earthly paradise.

ALLITERATION

Draw a circle around the consonant sounds that are repeated in lines 37, 40, 43, and 44.

RESPONDING TO THE POEM

Re-read lines 50–54. What image, or picture, do the words create for you in your mind? How does this image make you feel? Do you have any questions about this image?

_____

_____

_____

_____

_____

_____

_____

_____

_____

_____

_____

_____

Alliteration

Poets use sound effects to make their verse musical and to emphasize certain key ideas, feelings, and images.

Alliteration is the repetition of consonant sounds in words that are close together.

1. Re-read lines 1–5 of the poem. List four examples of alliteration in these lines. Draw a circle around the consonant sounds that are repeated. One example has been provided for you.

   example: Ⓚubla Ⓚhan

   _____

   _____

   _____

2. In this line from Alfred, Lord Tennyson's "The Eagle: A Fragment," circle the consonants that provide an example of alliteration:

   He clasps the crag with crooked hands;

3. Use alliteration to create a sentence of your own that describes a person or a place.

   _____

   _____

   _____

   _____

Vocabulary Development

Developing Vocabulary

Carefully read the definition of each word below. Next, read the sentence that uses that word. These sentences contain context clues, other words that help you understand the meaning of the word. Then, write a sentence of your own using the word. Be sure to include context clues in your sentence.

1. enfolding *v.*: present participle of *to enfold*, which means "to envelop, contain, or embrace."	The grandmother, enfolding her grandchildren in a warm embrace, beamed with joy.

• This verb is formed from the prefix *en–*, in this case meaning "so as to cover," and the verb *to fold*.

Original sentence: _____

_____

2. waning *v.*: present participle of *to wane*, which means "to dwindle or decline."	Waning in the west, the sun would set very shortly.

• Waning derives from the Latin *vanus*, which means "empty." Think of *waning* as meaning "becoming empty."

Original sentence: _____

_____

The Victorian Period
1832–1901

Peace and Growth: Britannia Rules

Many changes took place in Britain during the reign of Queen Victoria
(1837–1901). But unlike those of the early 1800s, these changes took
place in a mostly peaceful, stable environment.

5   The British Empire was steadily expanding. By 1900, Victoria was
queen-empress of more than two hundred million people living
outside Great Britain. Meanwhile, back at home, the Industrial
Revolution was creating new towns, new wealth, and thousands of
new jobs. Government reforms slowly gave middle-class and working-
10 class people more political power. Progress was being made.

The Idea of Progress

For many Victorians, progress meant improvements that could be
seen, touched, counted, and measured. For example, the historian
Thomas Babington Macaulay wanted the London streets to be free of
15 garbage. He wanted neighborhoods planned and houses numbered.
He wanted people to be educated enough to read signs. Although
some Victorians had lower standards than Macaulay's, most agreed
that society was improving itself.

The Hungry Forties

20 Although most of Queen Victoria's reign was peaceful, the first ten
years were troubled. Millions of people were out of work. There were
terrible working conditions in factories and mines. Children worked
such long hours that they were falling asleep on the job and getting
caught in machines.

25   In Ireland a famine killed almost a million people and forced
another two million to move. Some went to English cities, where
overcrowding was already a serious problem. In the slums of
industrial cities such as Manchester, twelve people might live in a
single room; 250 people might share two toilets.

Here's HOW

VOCABULARY

I know that the word *stable* in
line 4 has several different
meanings. One is "a building for
horses," and another is "steady
and strong." I think that the
meaning of *stable* in line 4 is
"steady and strong" because it
fits in with the word *peaceful*.
Also, there is nothing about
horses in that sentence.

Your TURN

VOCABULARY

In line 20, the word *reign* is a
homophone—a word that is
pronounced the same way as
another word but has a
different meaning. What words
can you think of that are
homophones for *reign*? What is
the meaning of the word
spelled *reign*?

_____

_____

_____

_____

_____

_____

_____

_____

_____

_____

The Movement for Reform: Food, Factories, and a Bright Future

30 During the 1840s, people held huge rallies to protest the government's failures. After the 1850s, the price of food dropped. Factories and railroads made clothing, furniture, and travel cheap. A series of

35 reforms gave the vote to almost all adult males and limited the length of the workday for children. State-sponsored schools appeared in 1870 and became compulsory by 1880. By 1900, more than 90 percent of the English population could read and write. Things were improving.

40 ## Proper Behavior and Authority

Many Victorians believed that they were improving morally, too. In fact, they were so concerned with proper behavior that the word *Victorian* now means almost the same thing as *prudish*—that is, overly modest and too proper. In books and newspapers, editors

45 deleted words that might be embarrassing. In art and fiction, sex, birth, and death were softened into tender courtship, joyous motherhood, and saintly deathbed scenes.

In the home the husband was king. Middle-class women were expected to marry and make comfortable homes for their husbands.

50 Unmarried women had few job opportunities. Working-class women might become servants, and middle-class women might become governesses or teachers. In literature the middle-aged unmarried woman was often a comic figure.

Many Victorians saw the hypocrisy behind all of this straight-laced

55 behavior. However, such behavior was slow to change because it, too, was seen as a kind of progress. Prudery and social order convinced the Victorians that they were in control—that they had evolved beyond the "immoral," revolutionary behavior of the last century.

Intellectual Progress: The March of the Mind

60 Dramatic advances in science fueled the Victorian mind. Humans began to understand the earth, its creatures, and its natural laws. Charles Darwin and other biologists put forward new theories about evolution.

VOCABULARY

Underline the words or phrases in lines 33–39 that describe or name *reforms*.

VOCABULARY

The meaning of the word *compulsory* in line 37 is "required." What was the result of making it a requirement to attend school?

_____

_____

_____

_____

VOCABULARY

I looked the word *hypocrisy* (line 54) up in a dictionary. It means "pretending to be what one is not." The hypocrisy described in lines 54-58 is that the Victorians pretended to be good because they thought that good behavior put them in control.

Some thinkers, such as Thomas Huxley (1825–1895), saw scientific and technological knowledge equally as useful for solving problems as the knowledge used by Victorians who built railroads and pushed for social reforms. These thinkers believed that problems could be solved by science, government, and human institutions, such as schools and churches. Huxley warned that humans could lose out—that the problems would remain or grow worse. But Huxley and others like him saw no reason that they would not win.

Questions and Doubts

Many Victorian writers reassured their readers that progress was being made, but others challenged this view.

Charles Dickens is an example of the latter. This writer lived out a popular Victorian myth: Through his own effort and talent, he rose from poverty to wealth and fame. The happy endings of Dickens's novels are equally mythical, suggesting that things usually work out well for decent people. But an unsettling idea lurks at the core of many of these novels. Some of Dickens's most memorable scenes show decent people—often children—being abused and neglected. Could such a world really be a world of progress? Was society really advancing?

Dickens also raised questions about the costs of "progress." He often described the smoke and fire of industrial landscapes. In 1871, the social critic John Ruskin noted a new phenomenon that we now call smog. This "storm-cloud of the nineteenth century," he wrote, "looks more to me as if it were made of dead men's souls."

From Trust to Doubt

Early Victorian writers trusted in a higher power. For them, the purpose of a poet or writer was to make readers aware of the connection between earth and heaven, body and soul. Midcentury writers changed their tune a bit, however. Some found it difficult to believe in an infinite power—especially given the miseries and injustices of society. Still others were saddened by what looked like the withdrawal of the divine from the world. In his poem "Dover

Beach," Matthew Arnold strikes the major note of much mid-Victorian writing. "The Sea of Faith," he wrote, has ebbed. The old certainties are gone, and the only new certainty is disbelief itself.

100   By the end of the century, this kind of thinking was widespread. Earlier Victorian writers such as Dickens had created worlds in which happiness was possible. But in the works of Thomas Hardy and others, the world becomes hostile. Lovers and friends are hurt and betrayed by human troubles (such as unfaithfulness and war) and
105 natural troubles (such as death).

Order Out of Chaos

Victorian writers had many different purposes: They entertained, informed, warned, and reassured. But two purposes stand out as uniquely Victorian. First, these writers wanted to make readers
110 wonder about reality. Second, they wanted to show that human beings could impose order on reality. A story or a poem might *say* the world was ugly and made no sense, but the poem itself could *be* beautiful and make sense to its reader.

No matter what its purpose, Victorian literature should be seen as
115 a part of its society, not as a voice apart. Both its readers and its writers sought to move the world forward. But they also struggled against the world's grand contradictions and harsh realities.

Major Changes in the Victorian Period

- Factories and railways made Britain the world capital of industry.
- The population of Britain's cities grew rapidly.
- Education improved, literacy increased, and the reading public grew.
- Advances in science gave people hope for human progress.
- The costs of industrialization were heavy. They included child labor, unsafe working conditions, and widespread disease.
- By the end of the century, people began to question the materialism of the age. They also became skeptical of "progress."

VOCABULARY

In lines 100–105, underline the words or phrases that describe situations that are *hostile* (line 103), or unfriendly.

VOCABULARY

What do you think is the meaning of the word *contradictions* in line 117? What smaller word in the word *contradictions* can help you figure out the meaning?

_____
_____
_____
_____
_____
_____
_____
_____
_____
_____

Ulysses

Literary Focus: Theme

The **theme** is the central idea or message of a story or a poem. A theme is not the same as the subject, which can be stated in a word or two, such as ambition, love, or old age. The theme is what the writer wants to say *about* the subject. In this poem, Alfred, Lord Tennyson gives us his view of the subject of old age.

Reading Skill: Comparing and Contrasting

People **compare and contrast** experiences to make sense of the world. We **compare** by looking at ways in which things are alike. We **contrast** by looking at how they are different.

Into the Poem

Ulysses (yoo LIH seez)—Odysseus (oh DIH see uhs) in Greek—is one of the Greek leaders who fought in the Trojan War during the 13th, or possibly early 12th, century B.C. That war lasted ten long years and resulted in the destruction of Troy. Ulysses' journey home to Ithaca was equally as long. You would think that after a life of adventure and horrors, Ulysses would want to finally rest. But in this poem, Ulysses wants to go on a final journey—another adventure. He knows he cannot regain his lost youth, but he is still looking for something more out of life.

Ulysses

Alfred, Lord Tennyson

COMPARING AND CONTRASTING

In lines 4–5, I can see that Ulysses contrasts himself with the people that he governs. He understands them—they are savages—but they do not understand him.

Your TURN

VOCABULARY

Re-read line 3 and the footnote for *dole*. Then, write a sentence using the word *dole*.

_____

_____

_____

_____

THEME

In lines 6–7, it looks to me like Ulysses does not want to give up the traveling that he did when he was young. He wants to go on living a life of adventure, even though he is an old man.

YOU NEED TO KNOW The aging Ulysses is recalling some of his past adventures, among them the battle for the city of Troy and his sea journey home to Ithaca. He longs for the exciting life he had when he was young—outsmarting the Cyclops, dragging his sailors away from the island of the Lotus-Eaters, visiting the island home of the enchantress Circe. He rejects the security of a settled life and wants to keep testing his limits—experiencing new adventures. Ulysses speaks of passing his responsibilities as a ruler on to his mild, reliable son, Telemachus (tuh LEH muh kuhs). Ulysses realizes, however, that the men he feels closest to are the sailors with whom he shared his adventures. It is with them that he wishes to set sail again in search of work that is of value—"of noble note."

It little profits that an idle king,
By this still hearth, among these barren crags,
Matched with an aged wife, I mete and dole[1]
Unequal laws unto a savage race,
5   That hoard, and sleep, and feed, and know not me.

IN OTHER WORDS It's not much use for a king with no work to sit by this unlit fireplace, among these bare, steep rocks. My wife is old. I give out unequal laws to savage people who eat and sleep and do not know me.

I cannot rest from travel; I will drink
Life to the lees.[2] All times I have enjoyed
Greatly, have suffered greatly, both with those
That loved me, and alone; on shore, and when
10 Through scudding drifts the rainy Hyades[3]
Vexed the dim sea. I am become a name;

---

1. **mete and dole:** measure and give out.
2. **lees:** dregs or sediment.
3. **Hyades** (HY uh deez): stars that were thought to indicate rainy weather.

For always roaming with a hungry heart
Much have I seen and known,—cities of men
And manners, climates, councils, governments,
15 Myself not least, but honored of them all,—
And drunk delight of battle with my peers,
Far on the ringing plains of windy Troy.

IN OTHER WORDS I cannot give up traveling. I will
live life to its last moment. I have enjoyed my life greatly. I
have suffered greatly, both with those that loved me and
alone—on shore and at sea during storms. I have become
famous. I wandered with a hungry heart. I have seen much
and known much—cities, the people who live in them, the
way they act, their climate, their government. They all
honored me. I took joy in going into battle with my fellow
soldiers, far away in the flat, windy land of Troy.

I am a part of all that I have met;
Yet all experience is an arch wherethrough
20 Gleams that untraveled world whose margin fades
Forever and forever when I move.
How dull it is to pause, to make an end,
To rust unburnished, not to shine in use!
As though to breathe were life! Life piled on life
25 Were all too little, and of one to me
Little remains; but every hour is saved
From that eternal silence, something more,
A bringer of new things; and vile it were
For some three suns to store and hoard myself,
30 And this gray spirit yearning in desire
To follow knowledge like a sinking star,
Beyond the utmost bound of human thought.

IN OTHER WORDS I am a part of everything I've
seen. Yet all experience is an opening through which shines
the part of the world I haven't yet seen, its edge forever

VOCABULARY

The meaning of the word
unburnished can be figured out
by carefully reading line 23.
Underline the words in line 23
that give you clues to the
meaning. Then, tell what you
think the word means.

_____

_____

_____

_____

_____

_____

_____

_____

_____

_____

_____

_____

_____

_____

_____

_____

_____

_____

_____

_____

Your
TURN

COMPARING AND CONTRASTING

Re-read lines 33–43, and tell how Telemachus is like or unlike his father.

_____

_____

_____

_____

_____

_____

Here's
HOW

VOCABULARY

In lines 44–45, "port," "sail," and "seas" all refer to the ocean. I think the word _mariners_ in line 45 refers to sailors, or people who go out to sea.

fading as I move. How boring it is to stop, to rust, not to be famous—not to shine in use! As if just breathing were really living! If I had more than one life, it still wouldn't be enough; and not much is left of the one life I have. But every hour I live brings new things to me. It would be horrible to shut myself up for years when my spirit longs to learn more, to go beyond the farthest edges of human thought.

This is my son, mine own Telemachus,
To whom I leave the scepter and the isle,[4]—
35 Well-loved of me, discerning to fulfill
This labor, by slow prudence to make mild
A rugged people, and through soft degrees
Subdue them to the useful and the good.
Most blameless is he, centered in the sphere
40 Of common duties, decent not to fail
In offices of tenderness, and pay
Meet[5] adoration to my household gods,
When I am gone. He works his work, I mine.

IN OTHER WORDS   This is my son, my own Telemachus, whom I leave to rule my island kingdom. I love him, and he is wise enough to do this work. He can slowly and carefully tame these rough people and gradually make them useful and good. He is responsible; he can be trusted to do all the ordinary tasks at home when I am gone—take care of people, worship the household gods. He does his work, and I do mine.

There lies the port; the vessel puffs her sail;
45 There gloom the dark, broad seas. My mariners,
Souls that have toiled, and wrought, and thought with me,—

---

4. **isle:** Ithaca (IHTH uh kuh), Ulysses' island kingdom off the west coast of Greece.
5. **meet:** proper.

That ever with a frolic welcome took

The thunder and the sunshine, and opposed

Free hearts, free foreheads,—you and I are old;

50 Old age hath yet his honor and his toil.

Death closes all; but something ere the end,

Some work of noble note, may yet be done,

Not unbecoming men that strove with Gods.

IN OTHER WORDS There is the harbor, the ship with the wind puffing out its sail; there is the great, gloomy sea. You, my sailors, who worked and thought with me—who faced both thunder and sunshine with a playful welcome and with free hearts and minds—you and I are old now. But old age still has its honor and its work. Death ends everything, but before it comes, we might still do some noble work, worthy of men like us who fought with gods.

The lights begin to twinkle from the rocks;

55 The long day wanes; the slow moon climbs; the deep

Moans round with many voices. Come, my friends,

'Tis not too late to seek a newer world.

Push off, and sitting well in order smite

The sounding furrows;[6] for my purpose holds

60 To sail beyond the sunset, and the baths

Of all the western stars, until I die.

It may be that the gulfs will wash us down;

It may be we shall touch the Happy Isles,[7]

And see the great Achilles,[8] whom we knew.

IN OTHER WORDS The lights begin to twinkle from the rocks. The long day is ending; the moon slowly rises; the ocean moans with many voices. Come, my friends—it is not

COMPARING AND CONTRASTING

How does Ulysses' attitude toward his companions contrast with his attitude toward his son?

_____

_____

_____

_____

_____

_____

VOCABULARY

Ulysses uses several different words for "the sea" or "ocean." These are words that don't always have that meaning. I can tell by the context that these words mean "ocean" or "sea." The words are *deep* in line 55, *sounding furrows* in line 59, *baths* in line 60, and *gulfs* in line 62. I think this use of different words for the ocean and sea makes the poem more interesting.

---

6. **smite . . . furrows:** row against the waves.
7. **Happy Isles:** in Greek mythology, Elysium (ih LIHZH um), where dead heroes live for eternity.
8. **Achilles** (uh KIHL eez): Greek warrior and leader in the Trojan War.

THEME

At the end of the poem, what do you think is Ulysses' message about growing old?

_____

_____

_____

_____

_____

_____

_____

_____

_____

_____

too late to look for a newer world. Push off with your oars; sit where you used to, and row together against the waves. My goal is still to sail beyond the sunset, beyond the reflections of the farthest stars, until I die. Maybe we will drown; maybe we will land on the Happy Isles and see our old friend the great Achilles.

65 Though much is taken, much abides; and though
We are not now that strength which in old days
Moved earth and heaven, that which we are, we are,—
One equal temper of heroic hearts,
Made weak by time and fate, but strong in will
70 To strive, to seek, to find, and not to yield.

IN OTHER WORDS Though much has been taken from us, much remains. And though we no longer have the strength that long ago moved heaven and earth, we are still what we are. Our heroic hearts, made weak by time and fate, still share one determination—to strive, to seek, to find, and not to give up.

Theme

The **theme** is the central idea or insight of a literary work. A theme is not the same as the subject of a work, which can usually be expressed in a word or two, such as ambition, love, or old age. The theme is the idea the writer wishes to convey about that subject—the writer's view of the world or revelation about human nature.

For each quotation from "Ulysses" shown below, write a sentence or two telling how the lines are especially important to the poem's theme of going forward and seeking knowledge. Number 3 has been done for you.

Theme: Never give up, no matter how old you are. Go forward, and seek knowledge and experience.

Passage from the Poem	Relationship to Theme
1. I cannot rest from travel; I will drink Life to the lees. (lines 6–7)	
2. How dull it is to pause, to make an end, To rust unburnished, not to shine in use! (lines 22–23)	
3. Come, my friends, 'Tis not too late to seek a newer world. (lines 56–57)	**3.** These lines show Ulysses as someone who who wants to go on adventures and make new discoveries.
4. Though much is taken, much abides; and though We are not now that strength which in old days Moved earth and heaven, that which we are, we are,— (lines 65–67)	

The Bet

Literary Focus: Theme

The **theme** is the overall meaning of a work of literature that usually expresses a view or comment on life. Writers rarely state their themes directly. The reader must consider all the elements of a story in order to piece together the possible meanings of the work as a whole. Because each reader brings different values and experiences to the story, interpretations will vary. This is especially true in an open-ended story like "The Bet."

Reading Skill: Making Predictions

A **prediction** is a guess about what will happen in a piece of literature. As you read, identify clues that hint at what will happen to the characters in the story. Then, use these clues to make predictions. As you read, you may need to change your predictions based on what actually happens in the story. Make note of the details that cause you to change your predictions.

Into the Story

This story is set in Russia in 1885. It begins with an elderly banker remembering a dinner-party argument fifteen years earlier. The banker and a young lawyer had argued about which was worse—life imprisonment or capital punishment (death). The lawyer claimed he would take life imprisonment, so the banker bet him he couldn't live all alone for five years. The lawyer took the bet, bragging that he could do it for fifteen years.

Anton Chekhov often wrote about exiles—people removed from their ordinary life or home—and strangers. In this famous story the lawyer chooses to exile himself, with interesting results.

Anton Chekhov

THE BET

BASED ON THE STORY TRANSLATED BY
Constance Garnett

It was a dark autumn night. The old banker walked back and forth, remembering a party he had given one evening fifteen years ago. Many clever men were there; at last, talk turned to the death penalty.[1] Most of the guests thought it was wrong. They believed it was

5 immoral[2] and unsuitable for Christian countries. Some even thought it should be replaced by life imprisonment.[3]

"I don't agree with you," said the banker. "I have not tried either one, but it seems the death penalty is fairer and more kindhearted. The death penalty kills a man at once, but going to prison for life kills

10 him slowly."

"Both are equally wrong," said one guest, "for they both want to do the same thing—take away life. The state is not God. It has no right to take away what it cannot give back."

A lawyer was among the guests, a young man twenty-five years

15 old. He said, "The death sentence and the life sentence are both wrong, but if I had to choose between them, I would choose imprisonment. Any life is better than none at all."

The banker suddenly hit the table with his fist and shouted, "It's not true! I'll bet you two million you wouldn't stay all alone in prison

20 for five years."

"If you mean that," said the young man, "I'll take the bet, but I will stay fifteen years, not five."

"Done!" cried the banker. "Gentlemen, I bet two million!"

"Agreed! You bet your millions, and I bet my freedom!" said the

25 young man.

And this foolish bet was carried out! The wealthy banker was delighted. He made fun of the young man, saying, "Give up this bet while you can. To me two million is nothing, but you are losing three or four of the best years of your life, because I know you won't stay

30 longer. I am sorry for you."

And now the banker remembered all this and asked himself, "Why did I make that bet? What is the good of that man's losing fifteen years of his life and my throwing away two million? Can it prove that the death penalty is better or worse than imprisonment for

35 life? No, no."

---

1. penalty (PEHN uhl tee): punishment.
2. immoral (ih MAWR uhl): wrong, wicked.
3. imprisonment (ihm PRIHZ uhn muhnt): putting or keeping in prison.

They had decided the young man should spend his captivity[4] in a little house in the banker's yard. For fifteen years the young man could not go out the door, see human beings, hear the human voice, or receive letters and newspapers. He could have a musical
40 instrument and books and could write letters, drink wine, and smoke. He could ask for these things in writing but could receive them only through a small window. Finally, the young man had to stay there exactly fifteen years. If he tried to break the agreement, he would lose, even if it was only two minutes before the end.

45 For the first year the prisoner was lonely and deeply unhappy. He played his piano day and night. He refused wine and tobacco. The books he sent for were novels with complicated[5] plots, exciting stories, and so on.

In the second year the piano was silent. Three years later music
50 was heard again, and the prisoner asked for wine. Those who watched him said all that year he did nothing but eat and drink and lie on his bed, yawning and talking angrily to himself. More than once they heard him crying.

In the sixth year the prisoner began studying languages,
55 philosophy[6] and history. He studied so much that the banker had to work hard to get him the books he ordered. In the next four years, he went through six hundred books and learned six languages.

Then, after the tenth year, the prisoner sat at the table and read nothing but the Gospels.[7] It seemed strange to the banker that a man
60 should waste nearly a year over one thin book that was easy to understand.

In his last two years, the prisoner read books of all kinds. He demanded, all at the same time, books on chemistry and medicine, novels, and some works on philosophy. He was like a drowning man,
65 desperate for something to hold onto.

The old banker remembered all this and thought, "Tomorrow at twelve o'clock he will be free. By our bet, I ought to pay him two million. But if I do pay him, I will have no money at all."

---

4. **captivity** (kap TIHV uh tee): time in prison.
5. **complicated** (KAHM pluh kay tihd): difficult.
6. **philosophy** (fuh LAHS uh fee): theory of knowledge and the nature of the universe.
7. **Gospels** (GAHS puhlz): in the Bible, the teachings of Jesus and the apostles.

Here's
HOW

MAKING PREDICTIONS

In lines 45-48, it says that the young lawyer was lonely and deeply unhappy during the first year of his sentence. It seems to me that his feelings of unhappiness will only get worse as time goes on.

Your
TURN

MAKING PREDICTIONS

In the lawyer's tenth year he became very religious. Do you think this means he will become happier? Explain.

_____

_____

_____

_____

Here's HOW

THEME

In lines 70-74, I can see that the old banker is desperate because he thinks that the only solution to his problem is murder! He seems to value money over all else.

Your TURN

VOCABULARY

The word *foul* in line 91 is a homophone, that is, there are other words that sound the same but are spelled differently and have different meanings. What homophone can you think of for *foul*? (Hint: The male crows and the female lays eggs.)

Fifteen years before, he had been rich, but gambling on the Stock Exchange and his own wild nature had lost his fortune. "Cursed bet!" muttered the old man, holding his head in despair. "He will take my last penny and enjoy life, while I will be a beggar and envy him. And then he will offer to help me! No, the only way I can keep from losing all my money is for him to die!"

The clock struck three o'clock. Everyone was asleep in the house. Quietly the banker took from his safe the key of the door to the young man's little house and went there. He called out to the watchman twice, with no answer, and decided that the man must be asleep somewhere.

The old man peeped through the little window. He could see the back and hands of the man sitting at the table. Open books lay everywhere.

The banker tapped at the window, but there was no answer. He turned the key in the keyhole. The rusty lock and the door creaked, but there was no other sound. He made up his mind to go in.

The man at the table was asleep. He looked as thin and bony as a skeleton, with long curly hair and a shaggy beard. His face was yellow; his hair was gray; you would not believe he was only forty years old.

The banker considered smothering[8] the man then and there. No one would suspect foul play.[9] But a paper on the desk caught his attention. He took up the paper and read:

"Tomorrow at twelve o'clock I have my freedom, but before I leave this room and see the sunshine, I must say a few words to you. I tell you that I despise all the things your books call the good things of the world."

"For fifteen years I have seen nothing of the world, but in your books I have drunk wine, I have sung songs, I have hunted in the forests, I have loved women. . . . In your books I have climbed mountains and watched the splendor of sunrise and sunset. I have performed miracles, killed, preached new religions, and conquered whole kingdoms. . . ."

---

8. **smothering** (SMUHTH uhr ing): keeping air from.
9. **foul** (fowl) **play**: murder.

"Your books have given me wisdom. I know that I am wiser than all of you.

105   "And I hate your books. I despise wisdom and the blessings of this world. It is all worth nothing. You have taken lies for truth and ugliness for beauty. You would be amazed if frogs and lizards suddenly grew on apple and orange trees or if roses began to smell like a horse. I don't want to understand you."

110   "To prove to you how I hate all that you live for, I give up the two million that I once dreamed of. To make sure, I will escape from here five minutes before time is up and break the agreement. . . ."

When the banker had read this, he laid the paper on the table, kissed the man on the head, and went out of the little house. He was

115 weeping. Never had he felt so great a hatred for himself. At home, his tears kept him from sleeping for hours.

Next morning, the watchmen ran in and told him they had seen the man who lived in the little house climb out of the window into the garden and leave. After checking to be sure that the lawyer was

120 really gone, the banker took the paper and locked it up in his safe.

Your
TURN

VOCABULARY

In line 105, there is a synonym for the word *hate*. (Remember that a synonym is a word that means the same as another word.) Draw a circle around the word in line 105 that is a synonym for *hate*.

Theme

The **theme** is the overall meaning of a work of literature that usually expresses a view or comment on life.

Answer the questions below to help you clarify the theme of "The Bet":

Questions to Help Clarify Theme	Responses (with Examples from the Story)
1. Does the title signify something about the story? Does it point to the truth that the story reveals about life?	
2. Does the main character change in the course of the story? Does the main character realize something that he did not know before?	
3. Are any important statements about life or people made in the story, either by the narrator or characters in the story?	
4. Is the theme ever directly stated? If so, where is it stated?	
5. In one sentence, state the story's theme. Do you agree with the theme? Is the writer presenting a truth about life or forcing us to accept a false view?	

Vocabulary Development

Column Match

For each word in Column A, write the letter of the correct definition shown in Column B. One has been done for you.

Column A

_____ **1.** sentence

_____ **2.** complicated

_____ **3.** immoral

___c___ **4.** smothering

_____ **5.** hate

Column B

a. wrong or wicked

b. time spent in jail

c. keeping air from

d. despise

e. difficult

My Sentence

Choose a word from the list above. Write a sentence using the word on the lines below:

_____

_____

_____

_____

The Modern World: 1900 to the Present

The Victorian age ended with the death of Queen Victoria, in 1901. At that time it seemed as if Britain's power and majesty would last forever. But political and social events during the early 1900s diminished Britain's strength. Several major colonies—Australia, South Africa, and New Zealand—gained their independence. Three things transformed British society: the increasing number of people who could read and write, the growth of the Labor Party, and new ideas about government.

Darwin, Marx, and Freud: Undermining Victorian Ideas

Many of the social changes of the early 1900s had their roots in the work of three men: Charles Darwin, Karl Marx, and Sigmund Freud. These thinkers helped overturn many of the firm beliefs of British society.

Darwin's *Origin of Species* (1859) sets forth a new theory of evolution. According to this theory, species that adapt to their environments survive, and those that do not die out. Some people tried to apply Darwin's theory to human society. These social Darwinists held that only the fittest people should survive. They used this idea to justify many unfair practices, including racial prejudice.

The German political thinker Karl Marx spent his last twenty years in London. In *Das Kapital* (1867), he argues that a society with large numbers of poor and few rich people is based on private ownership, and that all private property should therefore be done away with. This revolutionary thinking led to changes in many governments, including that of Britain.

In Vienna, Austria, Sigmund Freud changed the study of the mind. In *The Interpretation of Dreams*, Freud argues that human behavior is controlled not by our conscious minds, but by our unconscious desires. Some people were outraged by Freud's claims, but artists and writers found his ideas fascinating.

Here's HOW

VOCABULARY

The word *roots* in line 11 has many meanings. One meaning I know is "the part of a plant that begins under the ground." Because *roots* can mean a beginning, I think that is its meaning here. I can substitute the word *beginnings* for *roots* in the sentence and the meaning stays the same.

Your TURN

VOCABULARY

Underline the words or phrases in lines 15–17 that define the word *evolution*.

The Great War: "A War to End All Wars"

In 1914, all of Europe was plunged into World War I, also known as the Great War. At first, British patriotism ran high. Thousands of

35 young men enlisted. Six months later, thousands lay dead in the rain-soaked trenches of France. In four years almost an entire generation of young Englishmen was killed. With the end of the war, in 1918, came a new cynicism. The old values of honor and glory had led to war, a weakened empire, and a staggering loss of life. In place of those

40 values of the past, a bleak new realism settled in.

Artistic Experimentation: Shocking in Form and Content

Before the war, new trends in art had appeared. Henri Matisse was making bold use of line and color. Pablo Picasso was creating his first

45 cubist works. Igor Stravinsky was writing music that used strong rhythms and dissonant chords. Traditional ideas about beauty and order were being challenged.

After the war these trends led writers to see the world in different ways. In her novels, Virginia Woolf rejected chronological order and

50 experimented with shifting points of view. D. H. Lawrence rebelled against literary traditions and British prudery, shocking British audiences with descriptions of relations between the sexes.

Most influential of all was the Irish writer James Joyce. His novel *Ulysses* (1922), based on Homer's *Odyssey*, tells the events of a single

55 day in the life of a man named Leopold Bloom. In a wholly new way, Joyce drew from the deep wells of myth, symbol, and human imagination.

The Rise of Dictatorships: Origins of World War II

By the 1930s, another war seemed bound to happen. A worldwide

60 economic depression was helping dictators rise to power throughout Europe. Mussolini was dictator in Italy, holding control through brutality and manipulation. Germany fell into the hands of Adolf Hitler. He and his Nazi party convinced many Germans that Jews and other groups caused Germany's problems.

VOCABULARY

Cynicism (line 38) means "doubting." Therefore, a *cynic* is a person who doubts or distrusts people. He or she thinks that people are basically selfish. In lines 33–40, select two reasons that a cynic might have for doubting human nature.

_____

_____

_____

_____

_____

_____

VOCABULARY

I think that a cubist (line 45) would use cubism in his or her art because the word ending *ist* means "a person who does." I looked up *cubism* in a dictionary. Cubism is a kind of art in which natural shapes—leaves, faces, flowers—are broken up into geometric shapes—squares, triangles, circles.

65 Russia's Communist government was based on the theories of Karl Marx. In the 1920s, Nikolai Lenin had sought to do away with private property. Russia's next ruler, Joseph Stalin, sent as many as fifteen million people to forced-labor camps.

By 1939, Europe was again plunged into a bloody war. After the
70 fall of France, in 1940, Germany began bombing London and other English cities. The United States stepped in to help defeat Germany and its ally, Japan. On August 6, 1945, an atomic bomb was dropped on Hiroshima, Japan, by an American plane. The bomb ended the war, but it also wiped out the entire city. Small wonder, then, that
75 much of the literature following World War II was dark and unhopeful.

The End of the Empire

After World War II, the Labor Party came to power in Britain and transformed the nation into a welfare state. This meant that the
80 government provided its citizens with medical care and other basic needs. Britain suffered greatly during WWII and afterward had to focus on rebuilding its economy. Many of its colonies, including India, demanded and won their independence.

In 1998, an end to thirty years of violence in British-controlled
85 Northern Ireland seemed near at hand. The leaders of Northern Ireland, Great Britain, and Ireland hammered out a promising formula for peace. It was approved by most of the war-weary Irish citizens.

As a result of these and other changes, Britain's role in world affairs decreased.

90 ## British Writing Today

Preceding World War II, the politically radical poets W. H. Auden and Stephen Spender dominated the British literary scene. After the war, another group, known as the Angry Young Men, came into fashion. They disliked the intellectual snobbery of the Auden group. Many of
95 their works made fun of the newly wealthy middle class.

Since 1960, variety has marked British literature. In Britain, novelists such as Muriel Spark, Anthony Burgess, and Margaret Drabble have explored social issues and experimented with language.

The Growth of World Literature

100 Because of new technologies, writings in dozens of languages are now translated and spread throughout the English-speaking world. Many of these works point out the injustices suffered both in developing nations and in the West. Hundreds of writers from former British colonies explore the effects of cultural domination and racism. These

105 writers have seen their local cultures uprooted by foreign powers. They have had to ask themselves whether they should stay loyal to their native traditions, copy foreign ways, or create new forms of expression. Another complication for these writers is the fact that the English language is so common around the world. To reach the largest

110 audience, some writers from other countries feel that they must write in English—even if English does not convey everything that their native language does.

African Expressions

In Africa one response to oppression of native cultures was a literary

115 movement called negritude. Negritude encouraged black writers to use precolonial African culture, art, and history as a source of inspiration and pride. Although some writers believed that negritude was necessary, others felt that negritude idealized Africa's precolonial past. They felt that African literature must instead look at that past more

120 realistically.

Literature in India

In India, English is one of a number of languages used by writers. Two of the best known Indian novelists writing in English are R. K. Narayan and Anita Desai. Narayan is perhaps India's greatest

125 modern fiction writer. His characters often reveal a kind of stubbornness that is unique to India. Desai creates characters who must deal with many confusing social forces.

VOCABULARY

What do you think the word *injustices* in line 102 means? What clues in the word itself can help you to figure out its meaning?

_____

_____

_____

VOCABULARY

I think the word *precolonial* in line 118 refers to a time in the past when Africa was not ruled by others. The prefix *pre–* means "before." I looked up *colonial* in a dictionary and found out that it means "of a colony."

Copyright © by Holt, Rinehart and Winston. All rights reserved.   THE MODERN WORLD: 1900 TO THE PRESENT   **135**

Latin America and Magic Realism

In Latin America, writers have responded to their changing societies
130 in different ways. The Argentine author Jorge Luis Borges writes fiction that explores the nature of time and reality. His fiction contains stories within stories, character doubles, mysterious libraries filled with unreadable books, and parallel worlds that confuse and fascinate his narrators. Borges's works foreshadowed a literary style that came
135 to be called magic realism. This style combines realistic details with incredible events that are described in a matter-of-fact tone. Magic realists hope to surprise readers and make them question reality.

Women's Voices

One of the strongest voices to emerge in the postwar world is that of
140 women. Feminist writers address women's lack of power in a world controlled by men. In the influential feminist work *The Second Sex,* the French author Simone de Beauvoir analyzes women's secondary status in society and criticizes men for seeing women as objects. The Nigerian feminist Buchi Emecheta has influenced numerous women
145 writers from various African countries.

Responses to War and Government Repression

Since the beginning of the twentieth century, world history has been marked by periods of widespread warfare. Not surprisingly, then, much of modern world literature has been a direct response to war.
150 In *All Quiet on the Western Front,* the German author Erich Maria Remarque described the physical and mental horrors of World War I with such power that the novel was banned in Germany. Even more intense is the trauma experienced by the Italian writer Primo Levi and the Romanian writer Elie Wiesel during World War II's Holocaust.
155 Writers in the former Soviet Union, such as Aleksandr Solzhenitsyn and Anna Akhmatova, made an art out of going against government attempts to control their writing. Courageous writers, like Ha Jin (from the communist-controlled People's Republic of China), explore the unequal relationships between the government and the people.

The Modern World: 1900 to the Present

- New thinking challenged the beliefs of the Victorian age.

- The devastating "Great War" eroded the old values of patriotism and bravery.

- Artists began experimenting with new forms.

- Economic depression brought dictators to power in Germany, Italy, and Russia.

- Between 35 million and 60 million people died in World War II, including six million Jews at the hands of the Nazis.

- A weakened postwar Britain lost most of its colonies.

- Since the 1960s, many extraordinary writers have come from Britain's former colonies as well as other parts of the world.

In the Shadow of War

Literary Focus: Point of View

Point of view is the vantage point, or perspective, from which a writer tells a story. "In the Shadow of War" is told from the limited-third-person point of view. That means that the narrator is outside the story. However, the narrator does enter the mind of only one character—Omovo, who is eight years old. This means that the narrator cannot tell what other characters are thinking and must go where Omovo goes and understand only what he understands.

Reading Skill: Making Predictions

As you read this story, you are given a vivid picture of what the child, Omovo, sees and hears. Use the details you are given to think ahead and make **predictions,** or educated guesses, about what will happen to the characters. Of whom should Omovo be suspicious? Which characters seem dangerous? Jot down any predictions you make. Adjust your predictions as necessary while you read.

Into the Story

Ben Okri, the author of the story, was only eight years old when the Nigerian Civil War broke out, so it's not surprising that his main character, Omovo, is a child. The war began when the Ibo (EE boh) people tried to secede, or withdraw, from Nigeria and form their own state, called the Republic of Biafra. Thousands of people were killed in the civil war that followed, and many more died of starvation.

In the Shadow of War

BASED ON THE SHORT STORY BY

Ben Okri

MAKING PREDICTIONS

I think this story is told in a time of war because, in line 1, I see that soldiers come to the village. I wonder if there will be a battle in the story.

POINT OF VIEW

After reading the first four paragraphs of this story, I can see that the point of view is limited to what the main character, Omovo, knows and understands.

That afternoon three soldiers came to the village. They went to the bar and ordered palm wine and sat and drank amidst the heat and the flies.

Omovo watched them from the window as he waited for his
5 father to go out. They both listened to the radio. The news talked about bombings and air raids in the country.

At that hour, for the past seven days, a strange woman with a black veil over her head had been going past the house. She went up the village paths, crossed the Express road, and disappeared into the
10 forest. Omovo waited for her to appear.

His father gave Omovo his weekly allowance and said, "Turn off the radio. It's bad for a child to listen to news of war." Omovo turned it off. His father left quickly and walked to the bus stop to go to work.

Omovo sat on the windowsill and waited for the woman. The last
15 time she came, the children said that she was a witch—that she had no shadow and her feet never touched the ground. As she went past, the children began to throw things at her.

Omovo noticed that whenever children went past the bar the soldiers called them, talked to them, and gave them some money. He
20 ran downstairs. As he walked past the bar, one of the soldiers called him. He asked, "Have you seen that woman who covers her face with a black cloth?"

"No."

The man gave Omovo some money and said:

25 "She is a spy. She helps our enemies. If you see her, come and tell us at once, you hear?"

Omovo refused the money and went back upstairs. The heat got to him and soon he fell asleep.

When he woke, Omovo saw that the woman had already gone
30 past. The soldiers had left the bar. He saw them following her, weaving between the houses. Omovo ran downstairs and followed the soldiers. When they got into the forest, the soldiers stopped following the woman and took a different route.

Omovo followed the woman through the dense forest. She wore
faded clothes, with the black veil covering her face. She had a red
basket on her head. He completely forgot to look for signs that she
was a witch—whether she had a shadow, or whether her feet touched
the ground.

He followed the woman till they came to a crude camp near a
cave. Shadowy figures moved about in the half-light of the cave. The
woman went to them. He heard their tired voices thanking her. When
the woman came back she did not have the basket.

Again he followed her till they came to a muddied river. Omovo
saw the shapes of swollen dead animals lying on the dark water. A
terrible smell was in the air. Then he heard the sound of heavy
breathing from behind him. He recognized the voice of one soldier
urging the others to move faster. Omovo hid in the shadow of a tree.
The soldiers strode past. Not long afterward he heard a scream. The
men had caught up with the woman. They crowded around her.

"Where are the others?" shouted one of them.

The woman was silent.

"You dis witch! You want to die, eh? Where are they?"

She stayed silent. Her head was bowed. One of the soldiers
coughed and spat toward the river.

Another soldier tore off her veil and threw it to the ground. She
bent down to pick it up and stopped, kneeling, her head still bowed.
Her head was bald, and scarred with a deep groove. There was an
ugly gash along the side of her face. The soldier pushed her, and she
fell on her face and lay still. The lights changed over the forest, and
for the first time Omovo saw that the dead animals on the river were
in fact the swollen corpses of grown men.

Before he could react, he heard another scream. The woman was
getting up, with the veil in her hand. She turned to the second soldier,
pulled herself up, and spat in his face. Waving the veil in the air, she
began to howl dementedly.[1] The two other soldiers backed away. The
soldier wiped his face and pointed his gun at her stomach.

---

1. **dementedly** (dih MEHN tihd lee): in a crazy or insane manner.

Your
TURN

POINT OF VIEW

Using the limited-third-person
point of view, the author
permits the reader to see what
Omovo sees without analyzing
what it might mean. What is
going on in the paragraph
beginning with line 39 that the
boy is not mature or
experienced enough to
understand?

_____

_____

_____

_____

_____

Your
TURN

POINT OF VIEW

In lines 59–61, what is the
change in Omovo's point of
view? What does he see now
that he did not see before?

_____

_____

_____

_____

_____

_____

Your
TURN

MAKING PREDICTIONS

What do you think will happen to Omovo now that he has blacked out (lines 69–70)?

_____

_____

_____

_____

Here's
HOW

POINT OF VIEW

In the paragraph beginning with line 67, I can feel Omovo's terror. More than that, I fear for Omovo who may be in danger from the soldiers, who seem to be chasing him. I also understand that the woman with the veil is dead (lines 62-67). Omovo may not understand this because we only read what he hears, not what he sees. He hears a shot (line 67) and runs. He may have shut his eyes when he saw the soldier point his gun at the woman's stomach. It would be a terrible thing to see the soldier shoot the woman.

After he heard the shot, Omovo ran through the forest screaming. The soldiers tramped after him. As he ran, he saw an owl staring at him from the leaves. He tripped over the roots of a tree and blacked 70 out when his head hit the ground.

When he woke up, it was very dark. Thinking he had gone blind, he screamed, thrashed around, and ran into a door. When he recovered from his shock, he heard voices outside the room. He found his way out and was surprised to find his father sitting on the sunken 75 cane chair, drinking palm wine with the three soldiers. Omovo rushed to his father and pointed frantically at the three men.

"You must thank them," his father said. "They brought you back from the forest."

Omovo began to tell his father what he had seen. His father, 80 smiling apologetically at the soldiers, picked up his son and carried him off to bed.

Point of View

Because this story is told in the **limited-third-person point of view,** much is left to the reader's imagination. The reader must make inferences about what he or she is being told, because the events are seen through the eyes of a child.

In the left-hand column of the chart below, read how Omovo views events in the story. Then, in the right-hand column, explain how an objective third person, such as a reporter, might interpret that event. One has been done for you.

Omovo's Interpretation	Objective Observer's Interpretation
1. Omovo sees shapes of swollen dead animals lying in the dark water.	**1.**
2. Omovo's father tells him to thank the soldiers because they have brought him back from the forest.	**2.** The father wants to be on good terms with the soldiers.

Shakespeare's Sister

Literary Focus: Essay

An **essay** is a short piece of nonfiction writing that looks at a particular topic. Formal essays are impersonal in tone and tend to be full of facts. "Shakespeare's Sister" is an informal essay, showing the author's personal feelings, beliefs, and judgments about the subject of the rights of women.

Reading Skill: Identifying the Author's Beliefs

Identifying the author's beliefs helps you understand what the author's purpose was in writing the essay. Some of Woolf's beliefs will be stated directly. However, the author's other beliefs may be only hinted at. You will have to read carefully to interpret what she is saying about the role of women at a time when society was changing dramatically.

Into the Essay

In this essay, Virginia Woolf imagines that William Shakespeare had a sister, Judith, who was as talented as her famous brother. Woolf uses this imaginary character to comment on the differences between the treatment of women and men in Shakespeare's time— implying that women still face the same problems. In her writing, Woolf laid the foundation for our modern study of how cultural and economic forces help to shape the lives of women and men.

Shakespeare's Sister

BASED ON THE ESSAY BY
Virginia Woolf

Here's HOW

ESSAY

Based on lines 1-7, I would say that this essay will be about the unequal treatment of women and men in the Elizabethan age. From reading the introduction called "The Renaissance" on pages 50-55, I think the Elizabethan age was when Queen Elizabeth I ruled in England.

Your TURN

ESSAY

Woolf says that "It would have been completely impossible for any woman to have written Shakespeare's plays in the age of Shakespeare" (lines 10–12). Read lines 19–24, and then give one reason why this statement may be true.

_____

_____

_____

_____

_____

I find myself wondering why women did not write poetry in the Elizabethan[1] age. I am not sure how they were educated or whether they even knew how to write or if they had a place where they could write. They had no money, apparently, and most probably had
5 children before they were twenty-one. According to Professor Trevelyan, who wrote a history including the fifteenth and sixteenth centuries, they married at fifteen or sixteen.

Someone (I think it was a bishop who is now dead) declared it was impossible for any woman ever to have Shakespeare's genius.[2]
10 He was right in at least one respect. It would have been completely impossible for any woman to have written Shakespeare's plays in the age of Shakespeare.

Imagine, for instance, that Shakespeare had a wonderfully gifted sister named Judith. Will, her brother, went to grammar school,[3]
15 where he learned Latin, Greek, and logic.[4] He married and had a child. Then off he went to London, where he quickly became a successful actor. He lived at the hub of the universe. He met everyone, practiced his art onstage, and even went to the queen's palace.

Meanwhile, his extremely talented sister remained at home. She
20 had no opportunity to learn grammar and logic or to read the Latin poets. She was just as adventurous and imaginative as her brother and wanted to see the world as much as he did. But whenever she tried to read, her parents told her to mend the stockings or mind the stew and to forget about books.

25 Maybe she wrote secretly but was careful to hide her writing. When Judith was sixteen, her parents arranged a marriage for her— even though she protested that she didn't want to marry. Her father beat her severely and then begged her not to shame him. Although she felt she could not disobey him, one summer night she took a few
30 belongings and ran away to London.

---

1. **Elizabethan** (ih LIHZ uh BEE thuhn).
2. **genius** (JEEN yuhs): a very great natural ability of some special kind.
3. **grammar school:** a school where Latin was taught.
4. **logic** (LOJ ihk): the principles of reasoning.

"Shakespeare's Sister" adapted from *A Room of One's Own* by Virginia Woolf. Copyright 1929 by Harcourt, Inc; copyright renewed © 1957 by Leonard Woolf. Retold by Holt, Rinehart and Winston. Reproduced by permission of **The Society of Authors as the Literary Representative of the Estate of Virginia Woolf.**

Judith was as gifted with words as her brother. Like him, she stood at the stage door of a theater and told the manager that she desired to act, but he laughed in her face. No woman, he said, could possibly be an actress—in those days none were. So she had no way
35 to get any training in acting.

But she was young and pretty, so the actor-manager took pity on her. The result was that she found herself pregnant by him. One winter's night Judith killed herself and, as was common with suicides, was buried at some London crossroads.

40 That's how the story might go for a woman who, in Shakespeare's day, had the same genius that he had. But I think the bishop is right to say that no woman could possibly have had Shakespeare's genius then. For such a genius is not born among uneducated servants, and that is what most women, in essence, were. Women could not be
45 geniuses because their work began almost before they left the nursery, and law and custom forced them to keep on working. Only rarely do writers like Emily Brontë or Robert Burns appear from among the working classes.

Whenever you read of a witch or a woman possessed by devils, or
50 a wise woman selling herbs, or even a very remarkable man who had a mother, I think we are really on the track of a woman who wanted to be a novelist or poet but couldn't. It is women, I think, who wrote many of the poems attributed to Anon (Anonymous). Edward Fitzgerald, an English translator and poet, suggests women created the
55 ballads and folk songs, crooning them to children.

No one can say whether he is right. But I am positive that any extraordinarily gifted woman in the sixteenth century would have gone crazy or shot herself or ended up in a lonely cottage as half witch and half wizard. She would have been so mocked and so
60 frustrated that she surely would have lost both her health and her sanity.

No girl could have walked to London and forced her way before actors and managers without a great deal of anguish.[5] For women

---

5. **anguish** (ANG wihsh): great suffering.

Your TURN

IDENTIFYING THE AUTHOR'S BELIEFS

Read lines 43–48 to find the reason Woolf gives for her statement "But I think the bishop is right to say that no woman could possibly have had Shakespeare's genius then." Then, underline your reason.

Here's HOW

IDENTIFYING THE AUTHOR'S BELIEFS

Woolf believes that many women writers were never given credit for their work. They were the ones who wrote poems that are by "anonymous." I looked up *anonymous* (line 53) in a dictionary, and it means "without name."

Here's HOW

VOCABULARY

My teacher told me that Emily Brontë (line 47) is most famous for writing *Wuthering Heights*. Robert Burns (line 47) is famous for his poems written in the Scottish dialect. Both writers came from working-class families.

VOCABULARY

Read line 64, and then tell what the word *chaste* means. Circle the word in line 64 that means the same as *chaste*.

Here's
HOW

IDENTIFYING THE AUTHOR'S BELIEFS

After reading the paragraphs that begin with lines 79 and 85, I think that Woolf believes that writing is incredibly difficult. She names several things that can stop a writer from getting an idea down on paper. I have underlined these.

Your
TURN

IDENTIFYING THE AUTHOR'S BELIEFS

Woolf believes that women who wanted to write faced greater obstacles than men did. Read lines 90–97, and tell the special obstacles Woolf believed that women faced.

_____

_____

_____

_____

_____

were supposed to be chaste,[6] or pure. A sixteenth-century woman
65 living a free life in London and trying to write would have been under great stress that might have killed her. If she survived, whatever she wrote would have been twisted and deformed—the product of a guilt-ridden mind.

And if she managed to publish her work, it would have gone
70 unsigned. She would have published anonymously or used a man's name, as did Charlotte Brontë, whose pen name was Currer Bell. Throughout history, women have been made to feel that they should remain anonymous.

A woman born with writing talent in the sixteenth century would
75 have been terribly unhappy and would have had considerable inner conflict. Her life and her own instincts were hostile to the creative process.

But what mental state is most favorable for creativity?

Not until the eighteenth century did writers begin to record what
80 went on in their minds as they wrote. From their autobiographies, we learn that writing a work of genius is almost always unbelievably difficult. Everything—barking dogs, interruptions, money problems, poor health—conspires against having a work transfer easily from the writer's mind onto paper.

85 In addition, the world is incredibly uncaring toward writers. No one asks them to create novels, poems, or histories, for the world doesn't need them. Nor will people pay for what they do not want. So young writers must cope with every kind of discouragement.

Women who wanted to write faced much greater obstacles than
90 men did. To start with, no woman could have a room of her own unless her parents were very rich or noble. She had no money except what little she was given for clothes. So she couldn't go on a walking tour or a little journey to France, as Keats, Tennyson, and Carlyle, all poor men and writers, managed to do.

95 Even worse, the world was not just to women's writing as they were to men's. The world laughed at women who tried to write, saying, Write? What's the good of your writing?

---

6. **chaste** (chayst).

Identifying the Author's Beliefs

In "Shakespeare's Sister" one of Virginia Woolf's beliefs is that the way women were treated in traditional European societies prevented them from writing great works of literature.

Review Woolf's essay. Then, in the chart below, list five things about the lives of most Elizabethan women that would prevent them from producing great literature. One has been done for you.

Why Elizabethan Women Could Not Write Literature
1. Women could not go to school.
2.
3.
4.
5.

The Doll's House

Literary Focus: Symbol

A **symbol** is an object, an animal, a place, or a person used in fiction to stand for itself and for something broader than itself. Many symbols are widely recognized: A lion is a symbol of power; a dove is a symbol of peace. Writers often invent new symbols whose meanings are revealed in their work. In this short story the doll's house and the tiny lamp in it become powerful symbols.

Reading Skill: Making Inferences

Making inferences is a lot like being a detective. You use earlier experiences and knowledge as well as evidence from the story to make **inferences,** or educated guesses, about what is happening.

EVIDENCE FROM THE STORY
The wealthy Burnell children are given a fabulous doll's house.

KNOWLEDGE
I know what a doll's house looks like.

EXPERIENCE
I had a toy that symbolized comfort for me.

INFERENCE
The doll's house is a of wealth and prestige. SYMBOL

Into the Story

This story is set early in the twentieth century in a small village in New Zealand. At that time, New Zealand was still a British colony, with England's strict class system. In this system, people's status in society was automatically determined by their family background. People with inherited wealth and privilege did not ordinarily associate with poor, or even middle-class, people. In New Zealand, however, because of the shortage of schools, wealthy children attended school with children of different social classes.

The Doll's House

Based on the Short Story by
Katherine Mansfield

SYMBOL

After reading lines 11–14, I think Kezia is fascinated by the lamp because she likes small, seemingly perfect things. Perhaps to her the lamp symbolizes warmth or comfort.

MAKING INFERENCES

After reading the paragraph that begins with line 23, I understand that the Kelveys belong to the lowest class of people in the community. The other pupils do not "mix" with the Kelveys. An added detail is that many children are not even allowed to speak to the Kelveys.

When old Mrs. Hay went back to town after staying with the Burnells, she sent the children a marvelous doll's house. Because it still smelled of fresh paint, it sat in the courtyard, propped up on two wooden boxes.

5 The whole front of the house swung open, showing the living room, dining room, kitchen, and two bedrooms. Isabel, Lottie, and Kezia Burnell had never seen anything like it. There were pictures painted on the wallpaper, complete with gold frames. Red carpet covered all the floors except in the kitchen; red velvet chairs sat in 10 the living room; the beds had real bedclothes.

But what Kezia, the youngest of the Burnell sisters, liked more than anything was the lamp that stood in the middle of the dining-room table—a lovely little yellow lamp with a white lampshade. The lamp seemed to smile at Kezia, to say, "I live here."

15 The Burnell children hurried to school the next morning. They could hardly wait to tell everybody about their doll's house.

"I'm going to tell first," said Isabel, "because I'm the oldest. And I'm to choose who's going to come and see it first. Mother said I could."

20 Playtime came, and a crowd of girls surrounded Isabel. The only two who stood apart were the two who were always outside any group, the little Kelveys.

The Burnells lived in a rural area of New Zealand, where there was only the one school; therefore, their children had to mix 25 with children of all classes. However, the line on mixing had to be drawn somewhere, and it was drawn at the Kelveys. Many of the children, including the Burnells, were not allowed even to speak to them.

The Kelveys were the daughters of a washerwoman and a 30 father who was said to be in prison. They looked strange. Lil came to school in a dress made from a green tablecloth of the Burnells'; her little sister, Else, wore a long white dress and a pair of little boy's shoes. But whatever Else wore, she would have looked

strange. She was tiny, with enormous, serious eyes. Nobody had ever
35 seen her smile; she scarcely ever spoke. She always held tightly onto
Lil's skirt, so that wherever Lil went, Else followed.

Now they hung around at the edge of the circle of girls, listening
as Isabel told about the doll's house—the carpet, the beds with real
bedclothes, and the stove with an oven door.

40 When she finished, Kezia said, "You've forgotten the lamp,
Isabel."

"Oh, yes," said Isabel, "and there's a teeny little lamp that stands
on the dining-room table. You couldn't tell it from a real one."

"The lamp's best of all!" cried Kezia.

45 Isabel chose Emmie Cole and Lena Logan to come back with
them that afternoon and see the doll's house. All the others,
knowing they, too, might have a chance to see the house, were
extra friendly to Isabel. They crowded around her and walked off
with her.

50 The little Kelveys walked away; there was nothing more for them
to hear.

Days passed, and as more children saw the doll's house, the fame
of it spread. The one question was, "Have you seen the Burnells'
doll's house?"

55 "Mother," said Kezia, "can't I ask the Kelveys just once?"

"Certainly not, Kezia," said her mother.

"But why not?" asked Kezia.

"Run and play, Kezia; you know quite well why not," her mother
responded.

60 At last, everybody had seen it except the Kelveys. At lunchtime,
the children stood together under the pine trees. Suddenly, as they
looked at the Kelveys eating their jam sandwiches wrapped in
newspaper—always by themselves, always listening—the group of
girls wanted to be mean to them.

65 Emmie Cole started it. "Lil Kelvey's going to be a servant when
she grows up," she said.

"O-oh, how awful!" said Isabel Burnell.

Emmie nodded to Isabel in a meaningful way, just as she'd seen
her mother do on similar occasions.

SYMBOL

In lines 37–39, the writer describes how Isabel tells a circle of girls about the doll's house while the Kelveys stand outside the circle. What do you think the circle symbolizes?

_____
_____
_____
_____

MAKING INFERENCES

What can you infer about the characters of Kezia and her mother after reading lines 55–59?

_____
_____
_____
_____

Your TURN

SYMBOL

Re-read lines 65–81. What does being a servant symbolize for Lena and the other girls?

_____

_____

_____

_____

_____

_____

Here's HOW

MAKING INFERENCES

I think Kezia likes to do the opposite of what other people do or want her to do. She invites the Kelveys in to look at the doll's house, even though her mother says Kezia is not allowed to speak to them (lines 89–90). Another detail that is evidence for my theory is the fact that the other girls pick on the Kelveys at school and Kezia doesn't.

70 "Shall I ask her if it's true?" said Lena Logan.

"Bet you don't," said Jessie May.

"Watch! Watch me! Watch me now!" said Lena. She went over to the Kelveys.

Lil looked up from her sandwich, and Else stopped chewing.

75 "Is it true you're going to be a servant when you grow up, Lil Kelvey?" said Lena.

There was a dead silence. Lil only smiled her silly smile. This wasn't enough for Lena; she put her hands on her hips and shouted, "Yah, yer father's in prison!"

80 Then, Lena and the other little girls all rushed away, laughing and shrieking about the marvelous thing Lena had said.

That afternoon after school, Kezia was swinging on the big white gates of the courtyard. Looking along the road, she saw the Kelveys. Kezia stopped swinging as the Kelveys came nearer.

85 Finally, Kezia made up her mind.

"Hello," she said.

They were so surprised that they stopped. Lil gave her silly smile, but Else only stared.

"You can come and see our doll's house if you want to," said 90 Kezia.

Lil gasped; then she said, "Your ma told our ma you wasn't to speak to us."

"You can come and see our doll's house all the same. Nobody's looking," said Kezia.

95 But Lil shook her head still harder.

"Don't you want to?" asked Kezia.

Suddenly there was a tug at Lil's skirt and she turned round. Else was looking at her with big, imploring eyes; she wanted to see the house. So, like two little stray cats, they followed Kezia across the 100 courtyard to where the doll's house stood.

"There it is," said Kezia.

Lil took a deep breath; Else was still as a stone.

"I'll open it for you," said Kezia kindly. She opened the front of the house, and they looked inside.

105 "Kezia!" shouted Aunt Beryl from the back door, staring as if she couldn't believe what she saw. "How dare you ask the Kelveys into the courtyard!" she shouted in a cold, furious voice. "You know you're not allowed to talk to them. Off you go immediately!"

The Kelveys did not need telling twice. Faces red with shame,
110 huddling together, Lil and Else crossed the big courtyard and squeezed through the gate.

"Wicked, disobedient little girl!" said Aunt Beryl bitterly to Kezia and slammed shut the front of the doll's house.

When the Kelveys were out of sight of the Burnells, they sat down
115 by the side of the road. Lil's cheeks were still red with shame, but Else nudged her sister and smiled her rare smile.

"I seen the little lamp," she said, softly.

Then both were silent once more.

MAKING INFERENCES

I looked up the word *beryl* in a dictionary and found out that it is a hard and shiny mineral. Emerald and aquamarine are two varieties of beryl. Perhaps the writer used *beryl* for a name because she wanted to emphasize Aunt Beryl's hardness and cruelty (lines 105–108).

SYMBOL

What do you think the little lamp symbolizes for Else (lines 114–118)?

_____

_____

_____

_____

Symbol

A **symbol** can be a person, a place, a thing, or an event that stands both for itself and for something beyond itself. Listed below are some of the objects, people, and events that are present as symbols in "The Doll's House." In the first empty column in the chart below, tell what you think each item symbolizes in the story. In the second column, tell what else you think the item might symbolize. The first one has been done for you.

Item	Symbolism in "The Doll's House"	Other Symbolism
1. the doll's house	prestige and wealth also popularity for the Burnells	a family home childhood
2. the little lamp		
3. the circle of girls		
4. being a servant		
5. Aunt Beryl's name		

Write briefly about a person, a place, a thing, or an event that is symbolic for you.

_____

_____

_____

_____

Vocabulary Development

Developing Vocabulary

Answer each of the following questions. Then, write one or two sentences stating the reasons for each of your answers. Include context clues in your sentence(s) to show that you know the meaning of the italicized Vocabulary Word. Refer to the story if possible. The first one has been done for you.

Word Bank
propped
playtime
imploring
cold

1. If the doll's house is *propped* (line 3) up on two boxes, is it sitting on the two wooden boxes or beside them? It is sitting on the two wooden boxes.

   _____

   Explanation: The word up is used with the word propped. That means the doll's house is sitting up on the two boxes.

2. Is *playtime* (line 20) at the school a time to put on plays or a recess time? _____

   _____

   Explanation: _____

   _____

3. When Else looks at her sister with *imploring* (line 98) eyes, does she have a happy or begging expression in her eyes? _____

   _____

   Explanation: _____

   _____

4. When Aunt Beryl shouts in a *cold* (line 107) voice, is she coughing and sneezing with a cold, or is her voice unfriendly? _____

   _____

   Explanation: _____

   _____

AUTHOR AND TITLE INDEX